Praise from readers of *Saying Good*

"I just had to write this letter to let you know how much we as a family appreciated your book. My Mom was 86 when she came to live with us and my husband and I went through your book and planned everything in advance. She became sick a year later and during that time I could barely think straight, nursing her, day and night for a year. When she passed away, everything was all there ready for me just to go down the list and phone. We had done it all beforehand. Thank you so much for your book. It was a true blessing."

—Judy Woods, bookseller

"We couldn't have received a better gift. I don't know what we would have done without it."

—Lois Burge, retired teacher

Saying Goodbye with Love is a practical guidebook, written with sensitivity and providing straightforward, sound advice. I have personally used it as a resource and have recommended it to clients, often loaning my own copy. The book has proven to be an essential resource during the trying time when so many decisions are called for. I recommend *Saying Goodbye with Love* as an indispensable addition to your home library, where it will be a valuable friend when you need one."

—Richard T. Clarke, Psychotherapist

"Thank you for writing the book. My husband has done a lion's share of the estate and he's grateful to have a guide to help him along."

— Christine Jensen, farmer

"Thank you for your excellent book, which is now part of our Hospice Library. I will tout it to the heavens in my corner of the world."

—Jean Farina, hospice volunteer

"My husband and I are tremendously impressed with what you have done. Your wonderful book will relieve the sleepless nights of so many facing the death of a loved one, and the terrible anxiety of what to do when it happens. I particularly like the worksheets, which can be photocopied and ready for instant access."

—Jane Bailey, homemaker

"You cannot imagine what a godsend your book was since neither my brother nor I had ever been appointed before as an Executor. In the confusion and sadness of losing someone so close, it is impossible to think and deal with all that has to be done without some sort of guide. Your book provided all the necessary information as to what should be done and it is still being used as a reference."

—Priscilla Fong, office worker

Attention Corporations, Associations, Foundations, Professional Organizations, Colleges, and Universities:

If you are thinking of using this book for gift-giving, fund-raising, or education, quantity discounts are available on bulk purchases. We can also create special customized books, booklets, or book excerpts to fit your specific needs. For more information, write to: Special Sales Department, The Crossroad Publishing Company, 370 Lexington Avenue, 26th Floor, New York, NY 10017 or call 212/532-3650, extension 106.

Saying Goodbye with Love

A Step-by-Step Guide Through the Details of Death

Sheila Martin

A Crossroad Book
The Crossroad Publishing Company
New York

Saying Goodbye with Love

A Step-by-Step Guide Through the Details of Death

The Crossroad Publishing Company
370 Lexington Avenue, New York, NY 10017

First edition published by Sea Breeze Press in 1996.
This edition published by The Crossroad Publishing Company in 1999.

Text design by Sheila Martin
Back cover photograph by Bob Martin

Printed in the United States of America

Library of Congress Cataloging-in-Publication Data

Martin, Sheila, 1948-
    Saying goodbye with love : a step-by-step guide through the details of death /
  Sheila Martin.
        p.   cm.
    Includes bibliographical references and index.
    ISBN 0-8245-1585-4 (pbk.)
    1. Death—Social aspects—United States. 2. Death—Psychological
aspects. 3. Bereavement—Social aspects—United States.
4. Bereavement—Psychological aspects. 5. Funeral rites and
ceremonies—United States.   I. Title.
HQ1073.5.U6M37   1999
306.9—dc21   98-45462
                                                         CIP

1 2 3 4 5 6 7 8 9 10 03 02 01 00 99

Disclaimer

Dedication

Especially for Toni

Toni Theresa Alain
1952–1992
my dear, delightful friend and sister
I feel your love every day

And in memory of

Jennie Willard Sutherland Lindsay
1890–1984
the best of grandmas

Paul Brian Meagher
1953–1989
by the grace and passion of your dying,
you changed my life

Robert John Burge
1955–1995
Bobby, you climbed every mountain

Thank You

First, last, and always, heartfelt thanks to my beloved husband, Bob. It's a joy to walk beside you.

Love and thanks to my friend and sister, the late Toni Alain, for your loving heart and your unshakeable confidence in me.

Big hugs to my agent, Sheree Bykofsky, for believing in this book and in me. I love your "can do" attitude! And to Mike Leach, publisher *extraordinaire* for your wholehearted enthusiasm, not to mention your marketing savvy. Thanks too to the rest of the crew at Crossroad Publishing. Cheers to Tam W. Deachman, founding president of the Memorial Society Association of Canada and former funeral director, for reviewing the manuscript with such thoroughness. For expert assistance and advice, my thanks go to John Taylor, administrator of the Pacific Organ Retrieval for Transplantation program; Gordon Hardy, Executive Director, the Public Legal Education Society; James E. Houseman and the staff at Hamilton's Mortuary; and Peter Marshall, Memorial Society of B.C.

Thank you to the following businesses and professional associations who supplied me with helpful information: American Cemetery Association, Association for Death Education & Counseling, American Institute of Commemorative Art, British Columbia Funeral Association, Casket Manufacturers Association of America, Cemetery Consumer Service Council, Choice in Dying, Continental Association of Funeral and Memorial Societies, Cremation Association of North America, Dial-A-Law, Federal Trade Commission, Living/Dying Project, Lougheed's Limited, National Catholic Cemetery Conference, National Funeral Directors Association, National Selected Morticians, North American Transplant Coordinators Organization, Smith Services, Telophase Society, UBC Medical School, and Vancouver Crematorium. Also to Dr. John D. Morgan, Kings College, London, Ontario, and Derek Nuttall, CRUSE — Bereavement Care, England.

Many thanks to all the people from across North America who wrote or talked to me about their personal experiences as survivors. Some of their stories appear in this book. Hats off to Carl Dilley for sharing his very special story with me. And finally, to my dear Mum and Dad, Fay and Duncan Simpson, and to stalwart friends Helen Yeomans, Jeannie Bereziuk, Joanne Ingledew, and Perce Groves— all of whom cheered this project on during its earliest days—my warmest thanks.

A MOST SPLENDID FUNERAL

"When Chuang Tzu was about to die, his disciples expressed a wish to give him a splendid funeral. But Chuang Tzu said: "With heaven and earth for my coffin and shell; with the sun, moon, and stars as my burial regalia; and with all creation to escort me to the grave—are not my funeral paraphernalia ready to hand?"

—Chuang Tzu, *Musings of a Chinese Mystic*
(translated by Lionel Giles)

. . . .

Contents

The Tool Kit

14 ready-made forms to help you get organized

THE HAPPINESS OF DEATH

"The gods conceal from men the happiness of death, that they may endure life."

— Lucan

A Roadmap

Out of the Chaos

On March 13, 1984, at 6:13 in the morning, I awoke to the long-feared phone call. My grandmother, Jennie Sutherland Lindsay, was dead at the age of 93. Although we had known for many months that Grandma was dying, her death still came as a profound shock. What's worse, we were completely unprepared. Suddenly a mountain of difficult decisions and phone calls had to be made . . . immediately.

Are you prepared to handle the responsibilities when a death occurs?

Most people don't know what to do, and — just as unsettling — they don't know how to behave in the face of death. When death comes, you as a survivor must not only cope with your grief, but at the same time organize a major event, the funeral, which usually carries great significance — not just emotional, but social and financial as well.

What do you do first? And then what? How do you cope with the urgent decisions and details to be handled now and in the days and weeks ahead?

Saying Goodbye with Love is a down-to-earth guidebook for survivors who are responsible for handling the practical, legal and financial decisions that accompany a death in the family. You can use this book as a roadmap out of the chaos.

Upon first hearing of the death of someone you love, you may be hit by a whirlwind of emotions: waves of pain, fear, loss, horror, numbness, and confusion. You are in shock. You cannot think clearly. You fear making the wrong decision, or forgetting something important. In the midst of all this confusion, it is your job to organize the rituals of one of our most important rites of passage: death.

With *Saying Goodbye with Love* by your side, you'll be able to overcome the three key challenges of the newly bereaved:

1. **Fear of the unknown**

   Many of the decisions and details surrounding death are completely foreign to most of us. If you have never had to choose a casket, or plan a funeral service, or claim insurance benefits, the fear of "doing it wrong" can be overwhelming. The straightforward information and reassurance in *Saying Goodbye with Love* will relieve many of your fears.

2. **High stress levels**

   At the top of the standard rating scale used by psychologists to rate stressful life events is the death of a close family member. Much of the stress comes from a feeling of "falling apart," being unable to cope with the practical details.

   This book's checklists and forms will provide a structure to help you cope with these details. As well, the completed sections will give you a record of your progress through the stages of the crisis.

3. **The risk of regrets**

   Once life begins to return to normal, the survivors often have regrets. Perhaps they wish they'd organized the funeral differently ("We should have had them play that old Vera Lynn song that Dad always loved") or made different financial arrangements ("If only I'd known how much everything would cost") or written something more personal for the obituary.

   Because this guide includes so much concrete information and so many examples, you will be more likely to make choices which both salute the deceased and make your own future more workable.

Consider this: The dead are not in pain, but the living are. It's important for the survivors to receive help and comfort while going through the ceremonies of death. My goal has been to bring you knowledge of what your options are, and a realization that no matter what decisions you make, you are doing your very best.

Here is your chance to honor the one you have loved — by making the service a celebration of their life, by concluding their affairs smoothly and, finally, by grieving them well so you can get on with the rest of your life.

You will survive. And it is right and natural that you do so. My heart goes out to you now.

How to Use This Book

The ideal way to use this book is to read it while everyone you love is alive and well. If this is your circumstance, take time over the next few days or weeks to read through so you'll be able to make some of your decisions in advance. Then fill in as much of the written information as you can now — important names and phone numbers, vital statistics, and so on. Then spend some time working through Chapter 13, "Your Own Planning."

The "Tool Kit" included with the book is a set of fill-in-the-blanks forms you can use to help get things organized. Use as many of the forms as are useful for you. Or none at all. Feel free to make extra photocopies of any sheets if you need them.

Saying Goodbye is not meant to be a reference book that sits on the shelf. Instead, it's a tool to use at the time of death. The forms and checklists are only suggestions, not meant to be followed slavishly — simply a starting point to get you going.

Make this book work for *you*. Write notes to yourself in the margins. Add things. Cross out sections that don't apply or that you don't agree with. The only expert in your situation is you.

My assumptions

In writing this book, I've made several assumptions about you, the reader.

1. I assume you are reading this book to learn about organizing the service and disposition for a family member or friend. However, the information is just as useful if you are doing your own pre-planning.

2. I assume that the one for whom the arrangements are being made is already dead. If you are reading this book to pre-plan the arrangements for someone who is now dying, the references in the text to "the deceased" may be distressing. I do apologize. At the same time, I commend you for having the courage to deal with these issues before the actual death.

3. I assume you are organizing a medium to large service. For instance, much of the material on "Organizing Family and Friends" assumes you will have a houseful of people to deal with. But many services are small, just a few close friends and family. Again, use the information that works for you and ignore the rest.

4. I assume you belong to a Western religious group or that you have no religious affiliation. The practices of Eastern and Native American religions in coping with death are beyond the scope of this book.

5. I assume you loved the person who has died. Perhaps you didn't. Perhaps you and the deceased had resolved anger and hostility toward each other. Yet you still have to organize the service and all that goes with it. You have several options. Certainly you could find someone else to do the work for you. Or, you could see this event as an opportunity to begin your own healing of this relationship. Remember that anger can sometimes be an expression of love . . . we cannot be angry at someone we are indifferent to.

An invitation to you

Throughout this book, you will see anecdotes about the death experience, followed by a name and hometown. I am most grateful to those who took the time to write me. Now I invite you, too, to write to me with your stories about being a survivor of death. Or let me know how to improve and update the book for the next edition.

Please email me at *coachlady2@aol.com* or write to me in care of The Crossroad Publishing Company, 370 Lexington Avenue, New York, NY 10017. I would love to hear from you.

Chapter 1 ❧

What to Do First

You have just witnessed or learned of the death of someone close to you. What do you do first? Whom do you call? In this chapter you will learn about:

▸ What to do when death occurs

▸ Filling out the death certificate

▸ Phone calls to make right away

▸ Looking after yourself

▸ Five key decisions to make

What to do when death occurs

In North America today, the vast majority of deaths occur in hospital, and most of the rest occur at home. No matter where the death occurs, there are three activities that will take place fairly soon after the death.

1. A doctor must "pronounce death." In other words, the doctor must check for signs of life and make certain that there is no hope of reviving the person. Death may also be pronounced by a hospice nurse, the police, fire department, or coroner.

2. A doctor must decide the cause of death and sign the form registering the death, which is required for the official Certificate of Death. This may be the same doctor who pronounced death, or another doctor (for instance, your family doctor), or even the coroner or medical examiner. If there has been a long illness, determining the cause of death will be a straightforward matter.

3. The body must be removed from the place of death to the place where the services will be held or the body will be disposed of — usually a funeral home, crematorium, or medical institution.

If death occurs at home

❏ **If the death is sudden, call for emergency help**

If there is an accident or if death comes suddenly at home, call the fire department or paramedics immediately. (Someone who looks dead may only be unconscious.) Dial "911" for the Emergency Operator. Say you need immediate help, describe the symptoms, and give your address slowly and clearly. If the person is indeed dead, the coroner or medical examiner is legally responsible for finding out the cause of death. The fire department or police or doctor will call the coroner's office for you.

❏ **If the death is one that was expected, call the doctor**

If a natural and expected death occurs at home, call your doctor first. He or she must formally pronounce death. In many jurisdictions, the police must be called for *any* death outside a medical institution. Unless the death was a homicide or suicide, the police visit is a fairly routine matter. Ask your doctor to make the call to the police, if that is necessary, and to stay with you while the police make their investigations.

The doctor may sign the papers for the death certificate right away. If he or she does not, a funeral director or memorial society volunteer can help you complete the form and take it to your doctor for signing.

. . . .

A LAST GOODBYE

"When someone dies in a hospital or at home, instead of instantly removing their body, our group encourages loved ones to make their farewells before death has been disguised by the mortician's art. In the hours that follow death, the body feels cold to the touch, the color pales, but the facial expression softens. Peace is clearly evident. The process of grieving and the deepening recognition of love are continued beside the recently emptied vessel.

"Often when someone has died at home or in those hospitals where time is allowed with the body, we tidy up the room, put away the medicines and whatever life-support paraphernalia are about, dress the dead body in his or her favorite clothes, comb the hair, put on his or her favorite music, bring in some flowers, perhaps burn some incense, and allow those closest to the departed to come and pay their last respects and recognize how clearly that which they loved is no longer present. To see that who they loved was not just a body . . . . That consciousness has departed, and that is all."

— Stephen Levine, *Who Dies?*

. . . .

If death occurs in a hospital

❏ **Go to the hospital**

Eighty percent of deaths in North America occur in a hospital, nursing home, or hospice. If death occurs in an institution, the staff will call a staff physician or the patient's own doctor to pronounce death. At the same time, they will call you to come to the institution so that you may view the body, if you wish, and collect the deceased's belongings, including rings and jewelry.

❏ **Give instructions about what to do with the body**

Large hospitals usually have the facilities to keep the body for a day or so; smaller hospitals or nursing homes usually do not. In either case, the hospital will want to know your instructions as soon as possible about where to transport the body. If you are prepared, give the hospital the name of the funeral home or crematorium — or medical institution if you are donating the body. If you do not yet know what to do, tell the hospital staff you need time. Ask for the name and phone number of the person at the hospital to speak to once you decide. Say you will get an answer to them by a specific time.

Filling Out the Death Certificate

At the hospital, funeral home, or your home, the doctor or funeral director will ask you for information about the deceased so that a death certificate can be prepared. The death certificate, usually issued by the state or provincial government, is a legal document that has several purposes. It reports the cause of death and, later, it allows you to settle the legal and financial affairs of the deceased. After the form requesting a death certificate has been completed, it is taken or mailed to the appropriate government department, and within a few days the official death certificate is issued.

❏ **Gather the information for the death certificate**

Use the "Death Certificate Information" form on page TK 4 of the "Tool Kit" to gather the information you will need.

The information required where you live may not exactly match what is on the "Tool Kit" form, but it will be similar. If you do not have all the information — such as a parent's place of birth — don't worry. Most governments understand that some information may never be available.

Phone Calls to Make Right Away

There will be many calls to make over the next few days. These are the first ones. Record them here or use the Tool Kit form, "People to Call Right Away."

❏ **Doctor**

Name _____ Phone _____

Call your family doctor or the deceased's physician in the hospital.

❏ **A companion**

Name _____ Phone _____

If you are alone, call someone who lives nearby to be with you until other friends or family arrive.

❏ **A caretaker for the children**

Name _____ Phone _____

If there are young children in the home at the time of death, call their favorite sitter or a neighbor to look after them while you begin to make arrangements. Even older children may need some extra, loving attention.

❏ **Minister, priest, rabbi or other spiritual leader**
Name _____ Phone _____
Most clergy will be glad to take your call, even if you have not been a regular member of the congregation.

❏ **Executor and/or trustee of the estate**
Name _____ Phone _____
If you are not the executor, but you know the name of the person who is, call as soon as you can. The deceased's will may include information such as instructions for bequeathal of the body or preferences for the service.

❏ **Funeral home, memorial society, or crematorium**
Name _____ Phone _____
If you want to use a funeral home and have not already chosen one, see "Choosing a Funeral Director" in Chapter 8.

Important note: If you don't want the body embalmed, say so when you make this call. In some communities, embalming will be done automatically, unless you expressly request that it not be done.

Looking After Yourself

Even if you have been expecting this death, the irrevocable reality can still come as a profound shock. You may feel an overwhelming sense of aloneness and loss. You may feel anger, or stunned disbelief. You may be filled with manic energy, or feel as if you are moving in slow motion. You may experience an upset stomach, diarrhea, tightness in the throat, or shortness of breath. At a time like this, any reaction is possible. To cope with your stress, follow these guidelines over the next few days.

1. **Keep warm**
   The shock of a loved one's death may cause your body temperature to lower, leaving you more susceptible to colds and flu. Dress warmly, and tuck a blanket around you whenever you lie down.

2. **Rest**
   Whenever you can, sit instead of standing; lie down instead of sitting. Take 10-minute cat naps. Even if you don't sleep, it is good to close your eyes and still your body for a moment.

3. **Eat as much and as nutritiously as you can**
   At first, a glass of brandy may be just what you need to calm your nerves. But too much alcohol or caffeine will only add to your stress.

Do you have a food that spells comfort to you? Maybe it's hot chocolate, a peanut butter sandwich, or a big bowl of soup. If you don't feel like eating, drink fruit and vegetable juices throughout the day to keep up your strength.

4. **Breathe**

   In times of stress, we tend to hold our breath, which leaves us even more tired and anxious. Here is an easy way to calm yourself. Close your eyes for a moment. Be aware of your breath going in and out, in and out. Now, breathe a little deeper. With every inhalation, imagine that you are breathing in peace . . . calmness . . . acceptance. Feel it flowing through you, warming you and relaxing you. With every exhalation, imagine that all the pain and fear are flowing out of your body. On each in-breath, say to yourself, "I am breathing in peace." On each out-breath, say, "I am breathing out tension." You might even want to imagine yourself breathing in one color (a soothing green or calming blue) and breathing out another (an angry red or the grey of despair).

5. **Let others care for you**

   Let someone massage your neck and shoulders, or draw you a warm bath, or just be there to listen. Don't be afraid to talk about the deceased, about the death, or about your feelings. You are giving a special gift to others by allowing them to support you now.

Five Key Decisions to Make

Among the many decisions you will be making in the next few days, there are five important questions.

1. **Will any organs be donated, or is the body to be bequeathed to a medical institution?**

   If you haven't already decided, you'll learn about your options in Chapter 2, "Taking Care of the Body."

2. **Will you hold a service?**

   Chapter 4, "Planning the Service," has the details.

3. **Will the body be buried or cremated?**

   See Chapter 5, "Planning the Burial or Cremation."

4. **Will there be a visitation and/or viewing of the body?**

   Chapter 6, "Visitation and Viewing," looks at the choices.

5. **How much money will you spend?**

   For a discussion of this often difficult issue, turn to Chapter 7, "Estimating Your Costs."

LIKE A FALLING STAR

"Those who have the strength and the love to sit with a dying patient in the silence that goes beyond words will know that this moment is neither frightening nor painful. . . . Watching a peaceful death is like watching a falling star."

—Elizabeth Kubler-Ross, *On Death and Dying*

Chapter 2 ❧

Taking Care of the Body

Read this chapter to learn about

▶ The autopsy

▶ Transporting the body

▶ Organ donation

▶ Bequeathing the body

The Autopsy

In a small percentage of deaths, the question of an autopsy (medical dissection of the body) will arise. You may feel that your loved one has suffered enough: you want to spare him or her this final pain. But remember that the life (or spirit) is now gone from the body. The body can feel no more pain.

Why is an autopsy held?

An autopsy is held for one of three reasons:

1. **When required by the law**
   Although regulations differ from place to place, if death occurs without a doctor nearby, or under unusual circumstances, an autopsy by a medical examiner or coroner may be required by law. An autopsy is always required after suicide or violent death.

   During the autopsy, the examiners will look at various organs and tissues of the body to try to determine the cause of death. Because you have no say in the decision to hold an autopsy in these circumstances, you may feel power-less and angry. You may feel as if you and the rest of the family are under suspicion and somehow to blame for the death. But don't take the investigation personally. This is a routine matter. Look at it as being in the best interests of the deceased. It may be several days before the body is released — a stressful time for the survivors.

Important note: When there has been a suicide or violent death, the family, lover, and friends can suffer overwhelming feelings of rage, shame, and guilt. Without help, these feelings can linger for years. Many survivors have been helped by books and support groups, especially those that specialize in coping with your particular grief. Talk to your librarian, member of the clergy, or a community information referral service for recommendations.

2. **When requested to by the hospital and agreed to by the family**
   The hospital staff may request an autopsy to help evaluate the diagnosis or treatment given. If someone dies from a rare disease or condition, an autopsy might benefit medical research and improve treatments for other sufferers of the disease. If someone dies unexpectedly, even though of natural causes, an autopsy may further medical knowledge.

   In the case of natural death, no autopsy can legally take place without the family's permission. If you are asked to give permission for an autopsy, how will you decide? It can be heart-wrenching to think of this body you so recently held and loved now being examined by strangers.

   Many people make this decision by thinking of the autopsy as the deceased's gift to fellow sufferers. However, in this situation, the choice is clearly yours. If you find the idea too distressing, just say no.

3. **When requested by you**
   You may request an autopsy if you are concerned about either the diagnosis or the quality of care given, or if you have questions about the cause of death.

After the autopsy

If an autopsy is performed, the body will probably not be accepted for bequeathal or organ donation. If the death was violent, or if a full autopsy was carried out by the coroner or medical examiner, it may not be possible to have a funeral with open casket and viewing, but you can still have a closed-casket service. A hospital autopsy will usually be simpler. Clothing will cover any incisions.

When the autopsy is complete, the hospital or coroner will notify you or your funeral director.

❏ **Record any information you are given about the autopsy**
   If there is to be an autopsy, record any important information in the *Phone Calls Log* on page TK 9 of the Tool Kit. Include, for instance, the name of the coroner or doctor in charge, the phone number, what was agreed upon, and when the body will be released.

Transporting the Body

When a death occurs, the body must be moved from the place of death to the place where the service or disposition will be held. This may be a funeral home, crematorium, cemetery or medical school. Funeral directors often call this the "removal."

Note: Until a doctor has signed the registration of death form, the body cannot be moved. In many communities, only a licensed funeral director can legally transport the body. If you want to transport the body yourself — for instance, if you are taking the body directly to a medical school — you will need not only the death certificate, but a transportation permit. Ask the health department, coroner, memorial society, or a funeral director for information on local regulations.

If you have a long way to travel with the body, you may be required to have it embalmed or placed in a hermetically sealed casket before beginning your journey. For Americans, Lisa Carlson's book *Caring for Your Own Dead* provides a wealth of information on regulations and procedures in each state.

❏ **Record any information you are given about transporting the body**
If you will be transporting the body yourself, record any important information in the *Phone Calls Log*. Include, for instance, the permit required, where you apply for it, and the name and phone number of the person you spoke with.

. . . .

CARING FOR MY WIFE'S BODY

"For me perhaps the most important form of release was in personal involvement. I helped take care of my wife before she died, helped lift her body into the box, which we then loaded into my old station wagon. I then drove this myself to the burying ground, helped lower the box and recited her favorite poem about death. Generally, anything that survivors can do to care for the body or assist in services after death will help bring meaning and healing to the experience of bereavement."
— Ernest Morgan, *Dealing Creatively with Death*
(10th edition)

. . . .

Organ Donation

Across North America there is currently a waiting list of many thousands of would-be recipients for organ transplants. The organs that can be donated include the eyes, kidneys, heart, lungs, liver, bones, skin tissue, inner ear structures, and pancreas. While eyes, skin, and ear structures can be removed fairly easily after death, the solid organs (heart, kidneys, and so on) are difficult to retrieve in good condition.

In only a small percentage of deaths are the deceased's solid organs acceptable as transplants. The typical solid-organ donor is someone who has suffered brain death and whose heart and respiratory systems are being maintained by machines. Strict regulations govern the retrieval and transplantation of organs. The potential donor is always given exactly the same medical care and attention as those who have not experienced a wish to be donors.

If you are approached by someone in the hospital about donating the organs of a dying family member, you might consider it an opportunity to turn your tragic experience into a second chance for others. No matter what your decision, you can expect that everyone will be treated with the utmost respect.

All organs must be retrieved very quickly after death, so it is important to make the arrangements promptly. For more information on the decision to donate, see "Considering Organ Donation" in Chapter 13.

. . . .

THE DECISION TO DONATE

Carl Dilley, a White Rock, British Columbia stockbroker, tells of the death of his young bride, Betty, in September of 1988.

"She died of an asthma attack. It was a week after we got back from our honeymoon, three weeks after we got married. She'd had asthma for years, but it had never been a big deal. She had different sprays, and it was no problem. She was one of those people who is really fit and goes to aerobics all the time. You'd never think, ever, that that was going to happen to you.

She had a bad asthma attack and by the time the ambulance got her to the hospital she hadn't breathed for up to half an hour. They were able to maintain her on a respirator, but she was essentially brain-dead right from the start.

It was about four or five days later, that people started saying things like 'Well, we don't think she's going to get any better. She's in a coma, on the respirator.' It didn't even occur to me that she wasn't going to recover until she'd been in the hospital in the Intensive Care Unit for about four days. Apparently when someone suffers brain death, the conscious part is the part that's affected first, so you lose that virtually immediately and the part that controls your lungs and your internal organs is the sturdiest of the lot. And so that's the last to go. When somebody's in the state that Betty was in, she had to be maintained on a respirator because she couldn't breathe on her own.

As far as the organ donor thing goes, Betty and I had talked about it just after we got married. She'd bought me a new wallet — mine was pretty tacky — and she was putting all my credit cards in my wallet and she had my driver's license. She said, 'What's this little thing on your driver's license?' I said, 'That's to show I'm an organ donor.' She said, 'Well, when I get my new driver's license I'll do that too.' And that was all that was ever said about it. But I suppose it was enough for me to know that she felt good about the idea.

When the doctor first suggested organ donation, her Mom was pretty okay with it, but her dad — we went downstairs and were having coffee afterwards and he said, 'They're not going to do that to my little girl!'

I'd already thought about it. There's a million things you think about at a time like that and I thought: 'Well, okay, if she doesn't make it, that's one thing I'll do.' The people at the hospital didn't know what the program was at all. One of the things we didn't know was: Do they just leave her there until they find a suitable recipient? Six months? You have no idea what the process was at all. The hospital didn't know either. I talked to her parents again and they said, 'Okay, let's check it out.' Even though the ultimate decision was mine, I wanted them to be on-side.

Then the hospital rang up and they got John Taylor, the Senior Administrator of the B.C. organ retrieval program, to come to the hospital. He talked to us, her Mom and Dad, and her brothers and sisters, and myself. And John was just super. He handled it just beautifully. He, of course, had all the answers to all the questions. So we said, 'Yes, let's do it.'

I guess it was about 2 o'clock in the afternoon when the neurologist said, 'Okay, that's it.' They did the transplant operation at 5 o'clock Saturday morning.

Now there is a 23-year-old guy in Los Angeles who has the liver and there's a 28-year-old woman who has the kidney. Heart valves went to London, Ontario, and they used her corneas in the Eye Bank here. The liver recipient and the kidney recipient are both doing fine, and the man that got the liver wasn't expected to live. The girl that got the kidney had been on dialysis for years, couldn't work, and was in really tough shape. They're both fine now.

It surprised me at the time how logical I was about the whole thing. The ramifications of the whole thing didn't really sink in for a while. At the time I thought 'Okay, this is a good thing to do, let's just do it.' It wasn't some huge thing that was well thought out. But afterwards — out of something that's absolutely dreadful — you know, there's just nothing good you could say about it — this is one thing that's pretty good about it. So it's something I feel pretty proud of."

— Carl Dilley

In making this decision, your first task will be to find out if the deceased has expressed his or her wishes on the subject.

❏ **Look for a donor card**
Check the deceased's wallet or important papers for a card such as the Uniform Donor Card, Human Tissue Gift Act Card (Canada only), or similar document. Many states and provinces include identification of the desire to be an organ donor on the driver's license or medical CareCard.

❏ **Call the nearest organ retrieval organization**
If you don't know the organization's name or phone number, ask the hospital staff or your doctor.

❏ **Record any information you are given about organ donation**
If organs are to be donated, record any important information in the *Phone Calls Log*. Include, for instance, the name of the organization and the person you spoke with, the phone number, what was agreed upon, and when and how the body will be returned to you.

Bequeathing the Body

An alternative to organ donation is to bequeath (donate) the entire body to a medical or dental school. Although some schools have ample donations, many institutions across the continent are in urgent need of bequeathals, to help train new doctors and dentists, and to aid research.

If the body is bequeathed to and accepted by a medical school, only the eyes can be donated through an organ donor program. A body may be disqualified for medical-school use for various reasons, including contagious diseases, systemic infections, cancer, obesity, or mutilation. The gift may also be declined if there has been an autopsy, or if organs other than eyes have been removed.

Most institutions prefer to receive the body immediately after death. In some cases, it is possible to have a service with the body present before it is transported to the medical school. However, if the body is to be embalmed, the funeral director must follow the medical school's procedures (which are different from ordinary embalming).

It is best to arrange for bequeathal before death. See "Considering Bequeathal" in Chapter 13, for information on how to do this.

A CHANGELESS POWER

"I perceive that while everything around me is ever-changing, ever-dying, there is underlying all that change a Living Power that is changeless, that holds all together, that creates, dissolves, and re-creates."

—M.K. Gandhi

What to do at the time of death if the body is bequeathed

❏ **Look for a bequeathal certificate or donor card**
Check the deceased's wallet or important papers for a bequeathal certificate or card, which will give the name and phone number of the medical school, plus information about bequeathals.

If there is no bequeathal certificate, and you wish to find out whether bequeathal is still possible, ask your doctor, or memorial society volunteer.

❏ **Prepare a list of questions**
Your questions to the medical school might include these: Will they pay the transportation costs? On what day and time can they accept the body? Will the body eventually be cremated or buried? When? (It may be several months, or even years.) Will the ashes or remains be returned to you?

❏ **Call the medical school**
If the deceased filed a bequeathal certificate with the medical school, be sure to mention this on the phone. Although some medical schools always welcome bequeathals, others may decline for a variety of reasons.

The medical school may want to know the deceased's medical history, and other information that will help them understand the condition of the body.

❑ **Arrange for transportation of the body**

In most cases, it is the responsibility of the next of kin to have the body transported to the institution, although many medical schools will reimburse you for the cost of local transportation. The body can be delivered by the family (as long as you have the required permits), by ambulance, or by a licensed funeral director.

. . . .

SAYING GOODBYE TO TONI

My sister Toni died at home, almost three years after a diagnosis of brain cancer. The last few months had been increasingly painful, as she lost more and more of her functioning and the "self" that we knew seemed to drift away. The last little while she'd been unable to hear or see.

In spite of all that we'd been through, the stark finality of her death was a fierce shock. But a few hours later, some of us gathered in the bedroom for a final goodbye. After all those months of suffering, her gentle smile was extraordinary to see. Toni's husband, Phil, was there, her teenage sons Shawn and Jamie, my husband Bob and I, and Rosalie, who had begun as Toni's homemaker and ended as a devoted friend. We talked quietly, but easily, almost as if we were just there visiting Toni. Gittens the kitten played on the bed at her feet. The morning sun poured through the bedroom window. A rush of pure joy swept over me.

Although there have been many times of great pain and grief in the days and months since, that moment comes back to me often and always brings me peace.

—Sheila

. . . .

Chapter 3 ❧

Organizing

Family & Friends

Once word of the death begins to spread, the phone may ring constantly. People may arrive at the house, shocked and distressed. There is noise and confusion. You know you must call more people, make decisions, but you can scarcely think straight. You feel overwhelmed with the enormity of what must be accomplished in such a short time.

Even when it is expected, the actual death often puts us into crisis. But if you have others to help you, the burdens can be lightened. If no one volunteers, reach out and ask a few neighbors or friends for help. Most people truly want to help you; they simply need guidance. You can organize the efforts of family and friends so that everything comes together to create a fitting celebration for the life of the one you (and they) have lost.

As a first step — even before planning the service, writing the obituary, or meeting with the funeral director — it is wise to organize things on the home front. That's what we'll look at in this chapter. The topics are

▸ Who's in charge?

▸ Tasks to be assigned

▸ "What can I do to help?"

Who's in Charge?

Who arranges the service and related activities? A member of the family usually takes charge. Sometimes, though, a friend may be the best choice — at least for the administrative details.

Here are several recommendations to smooth your way. The first is the most important: Choose a chief. It is crucial that everyone understands and agrees on who's in charge; otherwise, friction and confusion can add to everyone's stress.

For example, if an older parent dies, each of the adult children may have a different point-of-view about how to make the arrangements. The spouses of those adult children may also want to give advice. Similarly, if a married adult child dies, the surviving parents and the spouse may have conflicting opinions about what should be done. Arguments within the family after a death can be bitter and long-lasting. If you can agree now to speak frankly with each other, you will all reap the benefits in years to come.

The "chief" may be one person, or it could be several people. At my cousin Bob's death, his younger brother, Kent and I easily shared this role and six of us came together to talk over the decisions. If more than one person is in charge, agree on your ground rules. Perhaps one person will look after organizing the service and cremation, another will oversee the household details, and a third will make the financial decisions.

The chief's main job, then, is simply to delegate. No one can do it all. More importantly, by giving other mourners the chance to contribute to the preparations, you are helping them to cope with their own grief.

Decide who will do each job best. Ask them whether or not they want to help with the task. And ask them to let you know when it is completed.

Tasks to be Assigned

The following list includes just some of the tasks. Use it to spark your own thinking about what you want done in the next few days.

You can use the blank *To Do List* on page TK 12 to prepare your own list of tasks for family and friends.

Around the home

✔ **Answer the door and welcome visitors**
If you like, use the *Visitors Log* (page TK 14) to record information about visitors. For example, "Knew Harry from school days" or "Offered to help with insurance."

✔ **Answer the phone**
If the deceased had many friends or relatives, manning the phone can be an emotional and exhausting task. If possible, have several people taking turns at this job. Two suggestions to smooth the way:

1. Keep the *Information for Callers* sheet (page TK 6) near the phone so you can answer callers' questions easily.

2. Have everyone use the *Phone Calls Log* (page TK 9) to record all important calls made and received. In the stress and confusion of these days, it is easy to forget who called and what was said.

   If a caller offers to help, and you have everything taken care of at the moment, ask if they are willing to help with something specific in the days and weeks after the service. Record their offer in the Log.

❑ **Organize child care**
Small children may need to be cared for, not just during the service, but before and after as well. If the one who died was the primary caregiver, you may need to begin looking for a permanent nanny/housekeeper.

❑ **Organize the food**
Shop for groceries. Cook for the family and visitors. Keep the kitchen clean. Find a large coffee urn. Plan food for the reception.

❑ **Look after housecleaning**
Housecleaning is especially important if the reception is to be held in the home. Specific tasks might include dusting, vacuuming, tidying, cleaning mirrors, doing the laundry, washing or waxing the floors, watering the plants, taking out the garbage.

❑ **Be responsible for family pets**
Pets may need to be fed, walked, and even comforted.

❑ **Help the mourners select clothing to wear at the service**
A suit or coat may need dry cleaning. Think about hats, shoes, underclothing, pantihose, and jewelry. In most communities, black is no longer essential, but simple, subdued clothing is considered a mark of respect.

❑ **Arrange hair appointments**
Perhaps you would like a hairdresser or barber to come to the house the morning of the funeral or the day before.

❑ **Polish everyone's shoes**

Other errands and tasks

❑ **Make a list of those you want to notify personally of the death, before the service**
In addition to family and friends, think of religious, social, business, or recreational groups, neighbors old and new, and school friends.

Use the *People to Call Right Away* list (page TK 7) to get you started.

❑ **Arrange accommodation for out-of-towners**
You might want to record the arrangements in *Accommodation Plans* (page TK 1).

❑ **Meet out-of-towners at the airport or station**
See *Travel Plans* (page TK 13).

❑ **Draw a map giving directions to important places**
Include the location where the service, burial, and the reception are to be held. This map does not have to be fancy, but it will be a big help, especially to out-of-towners. Can you fax the map ahead of time to those who might need it?

❑ **Find a photograph or other information for the obituary**
A photograph is certainly not necessary and it does add to the expense. If you do use one, it does not have to be recent. Why not use the photo that captures the person's spirit best? (Chapter 9 has details on writing the obituary.)

❑ **Chauffeur the family or visitors**

❑ **Arrange caretakers or support for those who need it**
Even when it is expected, death is a highly stressful event for everyone. Is there an older person who is strongly affected by this death, and who could use extra support right now? Is there anyone who might be at extra risk for health problems?

❑ **Order flowers**
Even if you have requested that others not send flowers, you might want some at the service. Homegrown bouquets can be especially lovely. If the casket will be present, what the florists call a "casket spray" of flowers draped across the top can give the mourners something beautiful to look at during the service.

❑ **Record gifts of food and flowers**
It is easier to record gifts as they arrive rather than trying to remember later. Keep track of them in the *Gifts Received* log (page TK 5).

❑ **Cancel any plans or appointments that need to be cancelled**
Check calendars — your own and the deceased's — for business meetings, medical appointments, and other commitments.

❑ **Arrange for special prayers or Masses to be said**

❑ **Make a list of distant friends and associates to be notified later**
Some people can be written to later or sent a printed notice of the death. See the *People to Notify Later* list (page TK 8).

❏ **Find someone to house-sit during the service**
An announcement of the time of the service in the obituary can be a temptation to thieves. Having someone to house-sit during the service will give you protection and peace of mind.

"What Can I Do to Help?"

At most deaths, one or more people are usually designated as the "primary mourners," for instance, the spouse, the parents of a child who has died, the adult children of an older person, or even a best friend.

If you are a friend or relative of one of the primary mourners, you can play a special role in helping that person through the difficult days ahead. It is not an easy role, and most of us have no training for it. Yet it is a wonderful opportunity to show your love for your friend.

Specific ways that friends can help

❏ **Comfort the children**
Even if they are too young to understand much about death, children can sense the pain and upset in the people around them. You may be able to give them extra hugs, or playtime, or just your quiet attention. Pets, too, need extra comforting.

❏ **Let the mourner talk**
You may feel that talking about the death is too painful for the survivor, that you should change the subject. But talking and expressing feelings are the very best therapies right now. If tears come, accept them. If the survivor simply wants to sit in silence, sit quietly with him or her. Your presence may be much more comforting than any words.

Encourage boys and men to cry, too, if that's what they're feeling at the moment. Those who try to be "brave" may pay a terrible price later in suppressed pain and anguish.

❏ **Listen, listen, listen**
Listen with your mouth shut and your heart open. Don't interrupt with your own stories, even though you think they may be helpful. At this moment, the mourner is only interested in her own story. She may say the same things over and over again, endlessly repeating the circumstances of the death, for instance, or replaying the last conversation. Keep listening. Don't interrupt. Don't offer advice. By speaking of her pain or talking of his disbelief, the survivor is slowly coming to terms with the death.

❏ **Write down your memories of happy times**
Often the condolences that are most appreciated by the bereaved are the stories of youth and laughter, reminiscences that share your appreciation of

all that was best in the deceased. Write those stories down so that they can be treasured again and again.

THOUGHTFULNESS OF FRIENDS

"My father died of a stroke late one night. I was twenty-five at the time, going to university, and the only child at home with my parents . . . . A thoughtful, unexpected thing that happened was that two of my father's friends (in their 60s, a lawyer and a university professor) invited me the day after the funeral to spend the day in their quiet, remote cabin outside the city, with the quiet talks, good meals and walks in the deep snow that were so refreshing and quiet after the talk and activity of the funeral and pre-funeral days."

—William Abraham, *Springfield, Newfoundland*

❑ **Avoid clichés**

Don't try to comfort with clichés: "At least she's out of pain now," or "You were lucky to have had so many good years together," or "You're still young; you'll get married again." Such "comfort" only causes fresh pain. Even phrases that sound comforting can be cruelly insensitive at a time like this. Avoid sentiments like: "It's a blessing in disguise," or "God wanted another angel," or "Time is a great healer."

Perhaps the expression that enrages mourners more than any other is the oft-heard: "I know just how you feel."

"How can you know?" the mourner wants to scream. "You don't have my memories, my shock, my anger at this terrible thing. Even if you have suffered through a death too, you don't know this death, this pain!" A simple "I'm sorry" may be best.

❑ **Let the survivor express anger or guilt**

Although it may be difficult for you, it is best to let the mourner verbalize feelings of anger ("Dan knew I hated his drinking. Why didn't he try to stop?") or guilt ("If only I'd been there when Vickie died"). These are normal, natural reactions to the shock of death.

If the anger or guilt continues for more than a few weeks after the death, you might gently suggest professional counseling or a support group. In fact, a support group is a good idea after any serious loss. Perhaps you can be the one to investigate the best local groups for your friend.

❑ **Do not minimize the loss**

To make light of someone's loss only causes further pain. For instance, if a child dies young or is stillborn, it would be cruel to say, "Well, at least you didn't have time to get to know him." You might say instead, "I know how much you wanted this baby."

Similarly, to compare the mourner's loss to another's is thoughtless and insensitive. For instance, you would not say to a young widower, "It's a good thing you only had a few years together. It would have been really hard if you'd been together 27 years, like Alice and me." A better comment would be: "What a terrible loss. You had so many good years ahead of you."

❑ Let the mourner be "crazy" for a while

In the early stages of mourning, the survivor may do seemingly irrational things, for instance, calling her dead husband's office to see what time he's coming home, or buying new toys for a dead child.

You may be anxious for the survivor to "face up to reality." Don't rush her. She may take many steps forward, sideways and back in the first months following a death. Your acceptance of her temporary craziness will help the healing.

❑ Offer specific help

Many people say to the mourner, "If there's anything I can do, let me know." It is usually better to make a specific offer, no matter how ordinary. For instance: "I can take the kids for a few hours Saturday, if you'd like some time alone," or "Would you like help filing the insurance claim?" or "When you're ready to go through Charlie's things, I'll be glad to help, if you want me to."

If you don't hear from the mourner right away, call and offer again. It may be too hard for him to call you, even though he dearly wants your help. Or he may have completely forgotten your offer, in all the confusion.

❑ Be there in the months to come

Time and again, survivors lament that people were helpful in the first days and even weeks after a death, but after that the silence was deafening.

If you can be the one in a hundred who continues to be there for your friend, you will have performed a great service. You may be rebuffed some-times — when the mourner just isn't ready to go out, or no longer wants to talk — but try to keep the door open. Your friend may appreciate your efforts far more than she is able to say right now.

. . . .

ADVICE TO FRIENDS

"To friends of the bereaved — go visit — call on the phone — they will let you know if they don't wish to talk but will know someone is thinking about them. Call every day if possible. It helps to pass long hours of loneliness with no mate to talk to, walk with or sit with at meal time."

—Marie Chapman, *Saint John, New Brunswick*

. . . .

❑ Honor your own feelings

Many of us are awkward and uncomfortable with death. If you have not experienced the death of someone close to you, it may be difficult to know what to say, or how to behave. It is normal to feel ill at ease.

The best advice is simply to be yourself. If you feel comfortable helping the mourner work through her emotions, do that. If not, put your energies into practical help, like mowing the lawn or making casseroles.

❏ **Realize it is okay to be angry at the change in your relationship**

It is natural for you to feel some resentment at the change in your relationship with the mourner. Perhaps you and he shared many interests and supported each other equally. Now it seems as if you are the one who must give, give, give, and your friend has no time to listen to your troubles.

If you are feeling resentful, take some time away from your friend. Find someone else to give you the support you need. Return to your friend only when you are ready.

❏ **Do your own mourning**

In your compassion for the primary survivor, you may be denying your own need to mourn. For instance, the father of a child who has died may be so concerned to support his wife that he puts aside his own grief. This may cause problems between them later, when each of them is at a different stage of grieving.

As soon as you can, find one or more people with whom to share your own grief and loss.

Chapter 4 ❧

Planning the Service

No matter what form they take, death rituals encompass two clear purposes: to help the living say farewell to the dead, and to dispose of the body respectfully. In this chapter we look at

- ▶ Thinking about the service
- ▶ The three types of service
- ▶ Combining a service and disposition
- ▶ Creating the service you want
- ▶ Writing the eulogy

Thinking about the Service

Many times people will leave a document describing their own wishes. It may be with the will or it may be in a document labeled something like "Letter of Instructions." Following those wishes will give you a head start on planning, if you are able to find them in time.

If you are thinking about a funeral or memorial service as the best way to say farewell, what are your goals for this service? Take a moment to write them down. Here is an example:

1. *To create a ceremony that celebrates Richard's life*

2. *To help myself and the other survivors express our grief and to comfort each other*

3. *To ensure that Richard's body is treated with respect and is disposed of as he would have wished*

Your own goals might include reaffirming spiritual values, or healing old family wounds, or even helping your loved one to make the transition from this life to the next. All the other choices you make — from the type of casket to the form of the ceremony — will be easier if your initial goals are clear.

Once your goals are clear, the next questions become: How can I best accomplish these goals? How do I turn these goals into a specific funeral or memorial service? Before planning the details, spend a few moments visualizing the kind of service you want.

1. **Start with a general picture**
   Will it be a quiet, simple leave-taking, or a large, colorful funeral? Something in between? Do you have any idea of how many people will want to come? Do you see it in a church or someplace else? Will there be music? Readings from the Bible or favorite books? A eulogy?

2. **Think about your reasons for choosing this kind of ceremony**
   If it is to be a minimal service, is it because that is how the person would have wished it? Because you want to keep the costs reasonable? Because the rest of the family prefers simplicity?

   If the funeral is to be grand, is it because your family always has large weddings and funerals? Or because the person was a great extrovert with many friends and acquaintances in the community?

   If your loved one took their own life, your first impulse may be to have a quick and private service. But a public service gives friends an opportunity to support the family and to express their own grief.

3. **Ask yourself whether you would prefer a different kind of service from the one you originally pictured?**
   Do you have other, more compelling reasons for making a different choice? Maybe you'd love to buy an expensive casket but it doesn't make financial sense. On the other hand, perhaps everyone in the family prefers a simple, no-frills service, but you feel you can best express your grief with a large, emotional ceremony.

   Keep asking yourself, "Who is this service for? Is it to please all our friends and relatives, or is it for me and my immediate family?" Remember that you may not be able to please everyone. Whatever feels right to you *is* right in this situation.

4. **Consider creative alternatives**
   What about a memorial service in a place that meant something to the person? For example, a special assembly in the school gymnasium for a teacher; a picnic in the park for the playmates of a child who has died; a tree-planting in honor of an avid gardener.

You might even have two services: for instance, a small, intimate ceremony at home for the family now, and a large, public event for the community in a few weeks, when you are over the initial shock.

· ·

THE RITUAL OF THE FUNERAL

"The ritual of the funeral was originally a skillful way of saying good-by to a loved one. It was a means of recognizing death. It was meant to encourage that which remains after the body has fallen away to continue with the work ahead: to go on in peace and stillness into the next perfect progression.

A funeral is an opportunity to acknowledge the love we have shared, as well as to remind the departed to continue on their journey without clinging to the life left behind. It is a way of reminding the departed to merge with their original nature, to let go of the particular and join with the universal. It establishes the balance between possessiveness and love, between pulling on the departed not to leave and wishing that being bon voyage. It is a ritual which encourages the heart to open to its grief as well as to trust in what exists beyond the senses."

— Stephen Levine, *Who Dies?*

· ·

5. **Evaluate your finances**

   It makes no sense to go into debt for a funeral or even to strain your family's cash flow. The expenses surrounding a death can add up to many thousands of dollars. See Chapter 7, "Estimating Your Costs," before making your final decision.

6. **Start with the idea that the service is a celebration — a thanksgiving for the life that was lived**

   What did this person love best about life? Make a list of favorite people, pastimes, and proud achievements: for example, raising three fine children, owning her own home, collecting comic books, dressing with style, belonging to the Rotarians, reading romance novels, enjoying several career successes, hiking in the wilderness, winning the hockey pool, graduating from college — whatever was a source of pride or pleasure.

   What were her most memorable qualities? (A razor-sharp mind, perhaps, or a lilting laugh.) His most interesting weaknesses? (An Irish temper? A fondness for all-night poker?)

7. **Think of ways to incorporate the things that made this person unique into the service or eulogy**

   For instance, you could set up a memorial table at the service or at the reception. On the table you can arrange significant objects, such as symbols of hobbies (a fishing rod or golf gloves), a child's favorite blanket, university diplomas, the career resume he was so proud of, her well-worn apron. Place a photograph and some flowers in the center of the display.

The Three Types of Service

There are three types of ceremony: the funeral service, the memorial service or service of remembrance, and the committal service. The traditional North American service includes some or all of the following elements: prayers, music, readings from scriptures or secular readings, a sermon or homily, silent meditation, one or more eulogies, and a final viewing of the body.

. . . .

ALLENE'S FUNERAL

"A lady in her middle 50s had been combatting cancer for about 12 years. The cancer was winning. This lady, whom I'll call 'Allene,' knew that she only had a short time to live. She called family conferences on a weekly basis to discuss her status and the latest information from the Doctor or Hospice Nurse. Toward the end she began to include me [her minister] in these conferences. The details of her funeral were discussed openly. She chose the Scriptures she wanted read and she chose the hymns she wanted sung and the special music she wanted presented and the person that she wanted to sing it. Nothing was left to chance and nothing was left to guess.

As I ministered to her (I saw her for a few moments every day), I was struck by her strong will and determination. She was not an educated person, having finished only the 8th grade, but she studied her disease and her medication and could speak with ease about what was going to happen to her. I noticed that she was the strong one through this whole episode and the people who came to visit her drew strength from her.

I mentioned to her that it seemed somehow unfair to have only me to preach her funeral. I asked her about an 'open mike' at her funeral. Basically, I explained, there would be a time when others could speak about Allene and how she had touched their lives.

Eventually Allene died . . . .

At the funeral I did not know what to expect when the time came for the 'open mike.' When I announced what we were going to do and sat down there was a time of silence. Then the Hospice Nurse rose and told about her relationship with Allene. One after another rose to remember Allene: a neighbor, a friend, her Sunday School teacher, others. Each spoke briefly, so as to not take time from the others. It was a very heart-warming time."

— J. Stuart Cundiff, *Goshen, Indiana*

. . . .

The funeral service

In a funeral service, the body is present; in a memorial service, it is not. For most funerals, a member of the clergy presides and the service is held within two or three days of the death. The casket is usually closed during the service, although it may be opened at the end for viewing. Following the service, the body is buried or cremated.

The memorial service

Although the body is not present during a memorial service, a viewing may be held beforehand. The body may be buried or cremated; disposition may take place either before or after the service.

You can hold a memorial service instead of a funeral, or in addition to it. For instance, you might have a funeral in the town where the person lived and died, and a memorial service later in the town where she grew up.

. . . .

A CELEBRATION OF HER LIFE

"My Mom had specifically stated in a will written years prior that she did not want a funeral or memorial service. We wanted to bring friends together in honour of my Mom (June Poirier), but wanted to remain in accordance with her wishes. We decided to have a 'Celebration of Her Life' and rented the church which June had attended a few times (Unitarian Church) and wrote out our own service. The service consisted of songs which were June's favorites, and which stressed peace and love. The service also stressed world peace and moving on toward the future.

The service was in a medium-sized room, and chairs were faced inward in an oval shape so that people could see one another, a very unique arrangement."

— Nicolle Poirier, *Regina, Saskatchewan*

. . . .

The committal service

The committal (or commitment) service is held at the graveside before the body is buried, or at the crematory before cremation. When held at the graveside, this ceremony is sometimes called the interment service.

Generally, only the family and close friends attend the committal service, which is usually brief. It may include prayers, music, or a reading. As a gesture of final farewell, one or more mourners may place a flower or a handful of dirt on the casket or in the grave. Some families stay to watch the lowering of the casket into the ground; many do not.

Sample ceremonies

Two excellent sourcebooks for ceremonies are Ernest Morgan's *Dealing Creatively with Death,* and *Humanist Funeral Service,* by Corliss Lamont.

Combining a Service and Disposition

There are six main combinations of service (or no service) and disposition.

If you choose burial, your choices are

1. **Direct burial**
   Direct burial means that there is no funeral or memorial service, although there may be a committal service at the graveside. In fact, if you want a ceremony with the body present, but without religious observances or viewing, direct burial with a graveside service may be your answer.

2. **Memorial service and burial**

   Since the body is not present at a memorial service, burial could be before or after the service.

3. **Funeral service and burial**

   This is the option chosen by the majority of North Americans. It is also the most expensive.

If you choose cremation, your choices are

4. **Direct cremation**

   Direct cremation means that there is no funeral or memorial service, although there may be a committal service at the crematory.

5. **Memorial service and cremation**

   Cremation could be either before or after the service.

6. **Funeral service and cremation**

   Because the body is present at a funeral, cremation must be after the service. Many crematories now have their own chapels where a traditional service may be held, or you may have the service elsewhere and then have the body transported to the crematory.

. . . .

SHOULD CHILDREN ATTEND THE SERVICE?

When children are involved, should they attend the service? Once again, there is no one right answer. Consider the child's age, understanding of death, and closeness to the deceased. Above all, remember to ask the child how he or she feels about attending.

"I was six years old when my grandfather died, and I adored him. Although I was young, I knew what death meant — I would never see my grandfather again.

As the funeral neared, my parents were discussing whether it was right for us children to attend. They decided that my brother and sister, who were seven and nine, were old enough to go; but I was too young.

I was devastated! I had seen my parents attend the funerals of friends and relatives, and understood that if you loved someone, you went to their funeral. If you didn't love them, you didn't go.

I somehow pictured in my mind that my grandfather would know who went and who didn't. The thought that he would know I wasn't there and would think that I didn't love him, was more than I could bear.

I threw tantrums for what seemed like months, always insisting that I was old enough. Finally, my parents gave in.

I sat in the front row and cried through the entire service. And, after some insistence, I even went to the graveyard to see his coffin lowered into the ground.

That was over twenty years ago, but I still brim over with emotion at the memory. Even though I don't think my parents ever fully understood my torment, to this day I am grateful that they gave in to their six-year-old child."

— Darlene Hanson, *Vancouver, British Columbia*

. . . .

Creating the Service You Want

If you are a churchgoer, you will probably be most comforted by the funeral rituals of your religion. Catholics usually celebrate a Requiem Mass; Quaker and Jewish funerals are usually simple and dignified, with no music or flowers. Protestant services often include the congregation reciting the Lord's Prayer. The rituals of faith can be comforting.

Yet even within the format of a religious funeral service, there is room for the special touches that will make the service most meaningful to you. Talk it over with your pastor or the funeral director.

❏ **Decide whether or not the ceremony will be religious**
If you don't know a member of the clergy, the funeral director will have a list, or you can ask someone you know who does go to church for the name of their pastor. Some ministers will agree to perform a nonreligious ceremony, if that is what you prefer.

❏ **Decide if you will have a military or fraternal order service**
If the deceased was a member of a veterans' association or fraternal order, you may want to follow their special service. Options may include a bugler, pall bearers or a Guard of Honor, or covering the casket with the flag, . Ask the officer in charge of such ceremonies to meet with you and discuss how to blend that ritual with your own unique needs. If you're using a funeral home, you can ask the director to contact the appropriate organizations and make the arrangements for you.

. . . .

A LEGION FUNERAL

"We planned a Legion funeral with all its Color Party — the casket draped with the Union Jack, a lone poppy on top. Both organ and piano were used — songs he loved were sung. The trumpeter played Reveille and the Last Post. He was buried in the soldiers' plot beside a pine spruce tree. He loved spruce trees."

— Tillie Howe, *Yorkton, Saskatchewan*

. . . .

❏ **Decide whether you want a public ceremony or a private one**
A private ceremony would include just an invited group of family and friends. A public ceremony is open to everyone. If the ceremony is to be private, decide who will be invited.

❏ **Decide where to hold the service**
Most services are held in a church or funeral chapel, but any place where people can gather together can be appropriate: a home, garden, by a lake or the ocean, on a boat, in an auditorium — wherever you will be comfortable.

If any of the mourners are handicapped, arrange for access or assistance at both the place of the service and the reception.

❑ **Decide on the time and date of the service**

A funeral is usually held within a few days after the death; a memorial service takes place days, weeks, or even months later. A morning or early afternoon service may be easier on you because it will be over earlier in the day. A lunchtime, evening or weekend service makes it easier for those who work to attend.

❑ **Choose the pall bearers**

If the casket is to be moved from the hearse to the front of the room, you will need pall bearers. Think of six or eight strong, healthy men or women who might want to participate. Don't ask anyone with heart or back problems.

When you meet with the funeral director, you can ask how much lifting will need to be done, and exactly how many pall bearers will be needed. (The size of the body and the weight of the casket are factors.) You might also want to choose some *honorary* pall bearers, who will precede the casket up the aisle but will not do any lifting.

You do not need pall bearers for a memorial service.

❑ **Choose the music**

With the music, you have many options. Will the music be live or taped? What selections do you want to hear? Will the congregation join in some of the songs or hymns?

When thinking about live music, think first about friends or family members who play or sing. They don't have to be professional musicians to contribute meaningfully to the service. If you do hire professionals, think beyond the traditional organist and soloist. What about a piper to pipe the casket in and out? Or perhaps a string quartet to play Bach or Brahms.

For a religious service, your choice of music may be limited to hymns and religious pieces (such as "Nearer My God to Thee" and "Amazing Grace"), but for non-church ceremonies you may consider other well-loved popular music. At my friend Paul's service, his brother and two sisters sang the old Dylan classic, "I Shall Be Released." (If you do choose a popular song, be sure that all the lyrics are appropriate for this occasion.)

Background music by artists like Zamfir and James Galway is often chosen to be played while people are entering or leaving. If you can't remember what songs the deceased liked, choose music that you like.

If possible, arrange for the tape equipment or musical instruments to be set up ahead of time so that volume and sound quality can be checked.

❑ **Choose the readings**

Readings can be from the Bible (such as the 23rd Psalm), or other books of scripture, or from writers speaking of death or love (such as Kahlil Gibran, Robert Terry Weston, or Tennyson), or from pieces written by family or friends. If you are lucky enough to have an appropriate poem or other writing by the deceased, that could make a memorable reading.

❏ **Decide whether or not to have flowers**
Flowers or greenery are soothing to many people. Even if you request "no flowers" from others, you may want to have a bouquet or two at the service, for the entrance and the altar. If the casket is present, you can place a simple spray on top of it, or blanket it with flowers. Arrangements from a florist give a formal, elegant look. Wildflowers or a bouquet from the garden are soft and natural looking.

❏ **Decide whether or not to have a memorial table**
A memorial table can be set up in the lobby of the church or hall.

❏ **Decide whether or not to prepare a printed program**
A printed program for the congregation can be a treasured memento. The program can list the events of the service and the words to any of the songs. Finally, the program can serve as a notice of death to be mailed to faraway friends and relatives.

As with everything else, there is no right or wrong way to put together the program. What about a photograph on the cover with a few words below? For instance: "Ruth in her garden on her 90th birthday," or "Harold and Maria on their wedding day, July 17th, 1946," or "Baby Jenny Kowalski, Jan.6, 1996 – Jan. 29, 1996. She lit up our lives."

A biographical sketch will be of interest to many. Write about the birthplace and other homes, children, grandchildren, honors received, and career highlights.

If a memorial service is to be held some time after the death, you can include tributes and remembrances from the letters of sympathy you have received. You might also include in the program the words of the eulogy.

❏ **Decide whether or not to tape-record the service**
Right now, you probably think you would never want to go through the pain of listening to the service again, but what about two or three years from now? That which is so painful now may turn out later to provide moments of quiet satisfaction as you are able to recall the loving way in which your partner, or child, or parent was mourned. A taped record can also be a precious gift in later years to any children who are now too young to understand this loss.

❏ **Choose someone to preside over the service**
Most funerals in North America are presided over by a member of the clergy. Funeral directors also perform many ceremonies. For a more informal service, a friend or family member may be a natural presider.

The job of the presider may include such things as deciding when to begin the service, leading the prayers, and reading from scriptures.

❏ **Decide who will ride in the funeral cars**
If there are to be official funeral cars, you may need the skills of a diplomat to decide who rides in which car. The immediate family usually rides in the first car; after that, there is no set protocol. If there is any chance of hurt feelings, plan and announce the funeral car arrangements ahead of time.

Writing the Eulogy

When my cousin Bob died tragically at age 40, it came as a profound shock to hundreds of people who loved him. We knew that with an open mike, dozens of people would want to speak and the ceremony would carry on for many hours, which just wasn't bearable. But we also knew that Bob was such a multifaceted person, that no one speaker could tell it all. At the service then, five of us spoke: a cousin from each side of the family, a representative of his company, and two friends. In the days following, groups of his friends gathered together at some of Bob's favorite surfing and climbing spots to tell more stories and relive their memories.

The term "eulogy" sounds stiff and formal, but a eulogy can include simple reminiscences, war stories, or favorite jokes. Here's how to put it together.

1. **Gather your material**
    First, collect the biographical facts: age, marriage dates, places lived, children, and so on. Now think about the stories you remember, or the turn of phrase or typical behavior that captures your loved one's character so well. Talk with other survivors, so the picture you present will include their ideas as well.

· ·

97 YEARS YOUNG

"Ruth was always interested in what was happening in the world and always looking forward with interest to something new to do, which gave her a timeless and ageless quality. (She was timeless in another sense too, as anyone knows who has ever tried to get her to a bus or plane or meeting on time.)

At age 75, after the death of her husband, she became a world traveler. In hospital, shortly before her death, the doctor said to her: 'You have had 97 good years, Mrs. Anstey.' Her reply was: 'But I haven't seen Vienna yet.'"

— Reverend Marvin Fowler, *eulogy for Ruth Anstey, Victoria, British Columbia*

· ·

2. **Come up with a theme**
    A theme gives unity to the eulogy, helping your listeners to see the rich patterns of this life. For example, let's say you are giving the eulogy for your late mother. As your theme, you decide to talk about your mother's ability to make a home wherever she hung her hat. Using this theme, you describe her English childhood, her eager arrival in Montreal as a shy, young war

bride, and then how she made a warm and welcoming home in every new army base to which your father's career took them.

Another example: Your eulogy for a friend might mention the various roles your friend successfully played: Raymond the Businessman, Raymond the Family Man, and Raymond the Winning Soccer Coach.

3. **Organize the material**

   Write your notes in point form on sheets of paper or on 3x5 file cards — one idea to a card. Now group the cards into piles of similar topics. Then sort each pile of cards into a logical order.

4. **Draft your speech**

   Write out the first draft of the text. (If you have access to a computer, use it to make your editing job easier.) Use linking sentences to make each topic flow easily into the next. Pay most attention to your beginning and ending. As you write and polish, keep the words "celebration" and "thanksgiving" in your mind. If it is appropriate, include a few moments of humor or light-heartedness.

A LETTER OF REMEMBRANCE TO MY MOM

This good-humored tribute from a married daughter was included in a booklet for family and friends produced in memory of a Montana woman, Ann Eck.

"Precious time has passed since I lost you, Mom. My grief for you has eased somewhat only because I know you stay with me in spirit. The most difficult thing I ever had to do was to say 'good-bye' to you. Even when you were alive, we always managed to cry at our farewells, but we both knew they weren't tears of sadness, but of a common bond of love and emotion that we shared. Many times when I phoned, you would say you were just about to give me a call or had been thinking about me!

You were always so supportive of my endeavors and activities even though they sometimes were a bit strange. How can I ever forget the time I flew home from college in Reno during spring break only to announce that my zoology class required collecting and 'preserving' small animal species. Having collected all my specimens in formaldehyde-filled jars, I couldn't possible take them back to school on the plane! So the next day you went down to the bus station and had them shipped to me. And when I called to let you know they arrived safely, you said the clerk needed you to place a dollar value on the 'cargo.' Remember your reply? 'Priceless — handle with extreme care — this is my daughter's semester grade in her college course and cannot be replaced!'"

— Karen Eck Banta, *San Jose, California*

5. **Practice the speech**

   If you are not used to speaking in public, borrow a book on this topic from the library and quickly skim it to pick up some tips. Read the speech into a tape recorder and then play it back. You'll be able to polish some more. Now stand in front of a mirror and imagine you are talking to your audience. Above all, remember to breathe.

If you are afraid you might break down while reading the eulogy, ask someone ahead of time to be ready to take over at a signal from you. Just knowing you have a backup will probably be all you need to stay calm.

If someone else is to give the eulogy

The pastor for a friend or family member may be the one to give the eulogy. If so, you can make his or her job easier by preparing some information.

1. **Write down as much as you can for the speaker — stories and reminiscences — even if it is not organized**
   Just telling him the stories may not be enough. Writing them down makes it easier for him to remember, and reduces the chances of misunderstanding or missing something important.

2. **Write out phonetic spellings of all the names that will be used**
   Write out the deceased's name, the survivors' names, and place names if the speaker is not familiar with them. It is distressing to hear a name or birthplace mispronounced during the service. For example, during the service for my grandmother, my late Aunt Inez's name was pronounced Ee-NEZZ. It should have been EYE-niss.

. . . .

WORDS FOR TONI

After my sister, Toni, died, I was physically and emotionally exhausted. I very much wanted to give the eulogy but had only a few free hours in which to write it. I didn't have time for writer's block.

My husband, Bob, took me out for our first-ever sail in our new ketch. It was surprisingly warm for the first week in April. While Bob steered, I found a quiet spot up front, closed my eyes, and talked in my mind to my sister. In a few moments, I began to write. The words came easily, almost as if I was taking dictation. And perhaps I was.

"Thank you all for being here with us today.

In the handmade card Toni sent to family and friends at Christmas 1990, she wrote: 'May Light, Love, Joy & Peace shine down on you in ever-increasing amounts. May humour always lighten your heart.'

Like her new-found assertiveness, her sense of humour was one of the things about her that grew stronger in the years of her illness. Even in the last difficult days of her life, Toni was forever coming out with the most atrocious one-liners!

Family and friends came above all else for Toni. Growing up, we had dozens of uncles and aunts and cousins. So many Christmases with the White Rock Simpsons. So many summers with the Burge boys. She knew how to celebrate special occasions and how to acknowledge special people in her life. Many of you, I know, received one of her hand-drawn cards, with caring words just for you.

Being close to her family was why it meant so much to Toni to die at home. Phil and Shawn and Jamie tore their hearts wide open to be able to care for her there. Gittens the cat helped too. What a gift to us all to be able to be with her at the end in that house on Wildwood Crescent which is so full of her things and her spirit.

The apple dolls, the spice ropes, and the giant teddy bears she fashioned during her craft fair days, the cookbook she and I created together, drawings everywhere, books everywhere . . . let's face it, lots of things everywhere. Toni was too busy living to bother overly much about neatness.

She adored her Phil and he adored her. What a love story, those two. And her sweet baby boys, Shawn and Jamie, grown now into fine young men. From the time she was five years old, Toni wanted to have babies of her own. She was so proud of her three strong men. And her love for Mum and Dad and I was fierce and unconditional.

Toni Theresa was surrounded by angels. She had angels to guide the surgeon's hands, angels to help her find the right words to comfort a friend . . . even washing-machine-repairman angels.

She was a deeply religious woman, devoted to the Virgin Mary, and the trip she and Phil and the boys took to Medugorje last year was one of the highlights of her life.

I'd like to read to you now part of something called the Song of Prayer. It seems to me to tell of how our Toni met her death.

'This is what death should be: a quiet choice, made joyfully and with a sense of peace, because the body has been kindly used to help this Child of God along the way she goes to God. We thank the body, then, for all the service it has given us. But we are thankful, too, the need is done to walk the world of limits. We no longer reach the Christ in hidden form, seen at most in lovely flashes. Now we can behold Him without blinders, in the light that we have learned to look upon again.

We call it death, but it is liberty. It does not come in forms that seem to be thrust down in pain upon unwilling flesh, but as a gentle welcome to release. If there has been true healing, this can be the form in which death comes when it is time to rest a while from labor gladly done and gladly ended. Now we go in peace to freer air and gentler climate, where it is not hard to see that the gifts we gave have all been saved for us. For Christ is clearer now; His vision more sustained in us; His voice, the word of God, more certainly our own. This gentle passage to a higher prayer, a kind forgiveness of the ways of earth, can only be received with thankfulness.'

And so we give thanks today for Toni's life and for the peace in which she walked towards death. What a price we pay when we love someone so deeply . . . and then lose them. But the price for loving Toni was worth it. Well, well worth it.

Go in peace, Baby Sister.

— Sheila Martin, *eulogy at Toni Alain's funeral, April 3, 1992*

LOVE SONG

The dead sing of nothing but love.

— Patrick Friesen

Chapter 5 🌿

Planning the Burial or Cremation

In this chapter you will read about

▸ Deciding between burial and cremation

▸ What to do if you choose burial

▸ What to do if you choose cremation

This may be a difficult chapter for you. It deals with decisions you must make about how to dispose of the body. As you make your plans, you might want to focus on the words by Ram Dass on the next page about the indestructibility of the human spirit.

Deciding between Burial and Cremation

Disposition is the final handling of the deceased's remains. Your choice is between burial and cremation — with variations on each.

Whatever you decide to do, the body will eventually return to its natural elements. Decomposition of the body in the earth is slow oxidation of the body tissues. Cremation, on the other hand, provides rapid oxidation. In cremation, the body is placed in a special furnace or chamber (sometimes called a retort) and subjected to temperatures of up to 2,000°F for two or three hours. With the intense heat and evaporation, the body of an average-sized adult is reduced to about five to seven pounds of "ash" and bone fragments. The cremated remains (or "cremains" as they are sometimes called) look like coarse sand mixed with broken bits of delicate white sea shells.

No casket is legally required for cremation, just a simple container, which is strong enough to hold the body. This could be a box of rough boards, pressboard, or heavy cardboard. Some crematories accept metal caskets; most require the container to be combustible.

Some definitions

A *columbarium* is a structure containing many spaces, or niches, where urns are placed. The columbarium may be a wall of a room, or an entire building. It may be part of an outdoor setting — a garden wall, for instance. The columbarium itself is constructed of long-lasting materials such as bronze, marble, granite, brick, stone, or concrete.

A *crypt* is a vault or chamber in which the body is entombed for above-ground burial.

A *grave-liner* is usually a wood or concrete box or concrete sections that are fitted together to form an enclosure for the casket. Its purpose is to prevent the grave from sinking. It is usually less expensive than a vault.

A *mausoleum* is a large, elegant above-ground structure or small building containing one or more crypts.

A *niche* is a recessed compartment in a columbarium. The niche may have an open front, protected by glass, or a closed ornamental front faced with bronze, marble, or granite. The urn containing the cremated remains (or some other memento) is placed inside the niche and the front is sealed. The dates of birth and death and the name can be inscribed on the front of the niche.

A *vault* is a container of metal, concrete, or fiberglass set underground, into which a casket is placed at burial. A vault is sometimes called a lawn crypt.

· ·

THE ADVENTURE OF DEATH

"There is an aspect of us — call it 'being' or 'awareness' or 'pure mind' or 'I' — that lies behind all the apparent phenomena (our body, emotions, senses, and thinking mind) which appear in the matrix of time and space. We intuit that even when we leave our body at death, this deeper part of our being is unaffected. With this basic change in identity, in the sense of who we are, death is converted from being a frightening enemy, a defeat, an unfortunate error in the universe, into another transformation through which we move, an adventure to surpass all adventures, an opening, an incredible moment of growth, a graduation."

— Ram Dass, *"Preface"* to Stephen Levine's *Who Dies?*

· ·

Burial choices

If the body is buried

1. It can be interred (earth burial).

2. It can be entombed in a crypt within a mausoleum (above-ground burial).

3. It can be buried at sea.

Additional burial expenses

If you choose earth or above-ground burial, there are related choices and costs.

▸ You may have to have the body embalmed.

▸ You will have to buy or make a casket (coffin) or burial box.

▸ For earth burial, the cemetery will probably require that you purchase a vault or at least a grave liner.

▸ You will have to buy a cemetery plot or mausoleum space. (A mausoleum crypt is generally more expensive than a plot.)

▸ There is a fee for opening and closing the grave.

▸ You may have to buy a grave marker or monument.

▸ There will be charges for annual or perpetual care of the grave site.

In parts of North America where the ground freezes in winter, bodies may have to be stored until the ground thaws in the spring. The cemetery manager may, however, estimate the number of winter deaths and dig a number of graves each year before the ground freezes.

Cremation choices

In general, funeral homes and crematories do not see cremation as an end in itself. The funeral director may urge you to "memorialize" the deceased by choosing a niche, crypt, or burial of the cremated remains. Here are your choices.

If the body is cremated

1. The remains can be stored by the family — and perhaps kept on display — in an urn or other container.

2. You may take the remains in the simple cardboard box supplied by the crematory and distribute ("scatter") them over land or water.

3. The remains can be placed in a niche within a columbarium.

4. The remains can be buried in the ground in a regular plot or in a smaller, cremation plot.

5. The remains can be entombed in a crypt within a mausoleum.

Additional cremation expenses

If you choose cremation, here are some other decisions and costs:

▸ You may want to purchase an urn to hold the cremated remains.

▸ You may want to purchase a niche in a columbarium with space for one, two, or the entire family.

▸ You may want to purchase a burial plot for the cremated remains — either a single burial site or a family plot.

If you are scattering the remains or distributing them in some way, there is no need to buy an urn, niche, or plot.

Do you know the deceased's wishes?

In the United States and Canada, the deceased's wishes regarding burial or cremation are not legally binding — even if they were written down.

After weighing all the factors — including the deceased's verbal or written requests, and the feelings of the primary mourners — it is up to the next of kin, or the executor or legal custodian to decide upon the method of disposition.

What does your religion say about cremation?

Protestants

Most Protestant faiths allow cremation, although some Lutheran and fundamentalist Protestant groups oppose it. Others, such as the Quakers and Unitarians, actively prefer cremation.

Catholics

Since 1963, the Catholic church has allowed cremation. However, tradition still strongly favors burial of the body. If you choose cremation, you may be required to bury the cremated remains in consecrated ground. Talk to your parish priest before making any arrangements. The church now allows a non-Catholic spouse to be buried in a Catholic cemetery next to his or her Catholic mate.

Jews, Muslims, Bahai's

Orthodox and Conservative Jews oppose cremation. Reform Jews see both cremation and burial as ways of respecting the body and protecting it from desecration. Muslims and Bahai's do not allow cremation.

Why people choose burial

Although the trend is moving toward cremation, the majority of North Americans still choose to bury their dead and to be buried themselves. Here are some reasons you might choose burial.

1. Burial is traditional within your family, religious group, or geographical area. For instance, in the United States today, about 79 percent choose burial. In Canada the rate is about 64 percent.

2. You do not like the idea of the body being "burned." You prefer to have the body slowly return to the elements.

3. You want to erect a monument on the grave.

4. You want to visit the grave in the days to come, and you find a graveyard more appealing than, say, a columbarium.

Why people choose cremation

In the United States, in 1972, only five percent chose cremation. That number had quadrupled by 1992. In Canada, the rate is now over 36 percent, in England 70 percent, and over 90 percent in Japan. The Cremation Association of North America projects that by the year 2000, one in every four Americans (25%) and 40% of Canadians will be cremated.

Those who choose cremation (for themselves or others) often hold the belief that it is better to honor the memory of the person, not the dead body. Here are some other reasons you might choose cremation.

1. Cremation is traditional in your family, religious group, or geographical area.

2. You prefer the body to be returned quickly and cleanly to the elements. You believe that a cremated body becomes one with nature more quickly.

3. You want to keep the costs down.
   Selecting cremation does not mean, however, that you will have an inexpensive funeral. You might still choose an expensive casket and/or a viewing, and/or decide to have the cremated remains buried in the ground or placed

in a columbarium. These choices can bring your costs up to those of a traditional funeral.

4. You have environmental concerns.
    Perhaps you are worried about the use of valuable land for cemetery space, or believe it is wrong to fill the ground with materials that won't erode: metal coffins and concrete vaults.

In 1985, the National Foundation of Funeral Service (an industry association including representatives from funeral homes, crematories, and related businesses) funded a study conducted by the University of Notre Dame, on the differences between those who chose burial and those who chose cremation. The study was called "Project Understanding" and was intended to help those within the industry know more about the potential buyers of their services.

The study found that the typical family member who chose cremation for a dead relative had more education, had a higher employment level, and was less active in religious affairs than those who chose burial. The study found no difference in the amount of caring for the deceased between the two groups. Some months after the death, those who chose cremation judged themselves to have recovered slightly better from their grief than those who chose burial.

Interestingly, affiliation with a Memorial Society had no bearing on the decision to cremate or to bury. Memorial Society members are as likely to arrange for burial as for cremation. Project Understanding found that the strongest influence on the choice for burial or cremation was the preference of the deceased.

. . . .

WORDS FROM A DYING MAN

"A dying man needs to die, as a sleepy man needs to sleep, and there comes a time when it is wrong, as well as useless, to resist."

— Stewart Alsop, *journalist, dying of leukemia*

. . . .

What to Do if You Choose Burial

Once you have chosen burial, there are other decisions to be made: whether or not to have the body embalmed, first of all, and choices about the casket, vault or grave liner, the cemetery, and the grave marker or monument.

Embalming

Embalming is a procedure whereby the blood is drained from the body and replaced with a preserving or disinfectant fluid, such as formaldehyde.

To *embalm* means to protect from decay. Embalming, however, does not preserve the body indefinitely. The more dilute the embalming fluid, the softer and more natural-looking the body. Stronger fluids can keep the body preserved for several years, but the body would not be suitable for viewing.

❑ **Decide whether or not the body is to be embalmed**

If there is to be a viewing, either before or as part of the service, embalming is a must. However, embalming is *not* required by law anywhere in the United States. For instance, if the body will not be present for the service or a viewing, and if it can be refrigerated until burial, there is no need for embalming. The legislation is not uniform in Canada, so ask your funeral director. It is, however, a requirement of most public transportation carriers that a body be embalmed before being shipped from one place to another.

Caskets

Since the casket (or coffin) is usually the most expensive item on the funeral bill, do think carefully about your reasons for choosing a particular kind of casket before going into the Selection Room of the funeral home. You will be better able to make a clearheaded decision — one not influenced by guilt or grief.

No casket will preserve the body indefinitely. No matter how well-sealed it is, no matter whether or not it is protected by a burial vault, the body will decompose.

Casket prices are based on factors such as how thick the steel is, or how many years the casket is warranted to keep moisture out. There is clear evidence, however, that sealed (or gasketed) caskets trap anaerobic bacteria, which cause the body to decompose even faster and less naturally than in an unsealed casket. Given that fact, perhaps a little rainwater getting into the casket is a lesser concern.

❑ **Decide what your needs are in choosing a casket**

A casket is a respectful way to carry the body in public. Beyond that, your choice fulfills an emotional need. For instance, do you feel that buying a special casket is a way to show your love for the person? Do you believe that a plain casket is more dignified? Is the casket a statement about his or her importance to the community?

Keep in mind that no matter how attractive a casket is, it is not doing anything for the deceased. The quilted pillows, spring mattresses, handpolished wood, or 12-gauge steel, the number of years in the warranty . . . none of these can be appreciated by the dead. Make your choice based on your own needs, not from the illusion that this is a "last gift" to the one you loved. Remember that your needs are different than your neighbor's, perhaps even different from those of the rest of your family. If there is disagreement, see if you can bring to light the beliefs and emotional needs of each family member. Once you understand each other's motivations, it may be easier to come to an agreement.

❏ **Decide what type of casket you want**

There are basically four types: the metal casket, the hardwood casket (usually highly polished), the cloth-covered softwood casket (usually covered in a pastel silk-like material), and the simple container. A metal casket may be made of steel, copper, or bronze. If you choose a metal casket and then have the body cremated, the body will be removed from the metal casket before cremation. (The casket is later broken up and turned into scrap.) Keep in mind that a metal casket will also be heavier for the pall bearers.

If you do not want a metal casket, there are usually several kinds of wooden caskets. There are also simple containers — for example, a corrugated fiber box or a plywood box. The funeral director is unlikely to have these on display, so ask to see them. Or call the crematory, which may have a better selection. If the container is to be displayed at the funeral, you may want to cover it with a decorative cloth or "pall" or a beautiful quilt.

❏ **Decide whether to buy a casket, rent one, or build your own**

Although the vast majority of funeral buyers do purchase a casket, that is not your only option. You can usually also rent a casket, or build a burial box. If the body is to be cremated after a funeral, some funeral homes will rent a casket for the service. Afterwards, the body is quietly transferred to a simple container which is used for cremation.

Ernest Morgan's classic book, *Dealing Creatively with Death,* includes cutting instructions and an assembly diagram for building a homemade plywood burial box. As well, you can buy plans for building cabinet-quality burial boxes. (See "Burial Boxes" in the Resources section at the end of this book.)

. . . .

IN A PLAIN PINE COFFIN

"We have a friend in Montana whose work as a carpenter is to make cradles and coffins. He also conducts simple funeral-burials. Often, in the back country, a hole will be dug and the body, in a plain pine coffin or perhaps just wrapped in tie-dyed cloth, will be lowered into the ground. Instead of a tombstone, a fruit tree is planted over that body. The roots nourished by the return of that body into the earth from which it was sustained. And in years to follow, eating the fruit of that tree will be like partaking in that loved one. It touches on the ritual of the Eucharist.

The funeral is a skillful means to remind the departed as well as those left behind that they are not simply a body. That there is so much more to life and living."

— Stephen Levine, *Who Dies?*

. . . .

Vaults and grave liners

For earth burials, most cemeteries require that the casket be placed in a protective enclosure — a burial vault or grave liner — which keeps the ground from settling as the casket disintegrates.

In years past, a fresh grave was left with a mound of dirt on top — about 18 inches high — which would gradually settle. Modern-day cemetery managers found it hard to use the new grass-moving machines around these mounds, and so established a requirement for some type of grave liner.

The funeral director may imply that a vault protects the casket. A vault may indeed protect against rainwater, but bacteria are still at work. Again, no burial vault or grave liner will preserve the body indefinitely.

❑ **Find out whether or not the cemetery requires a vault or grave liner, and decide which to use**
Nowhere in North America is a vault required by law. However, the majority of private cemeteries do require at least a grave liner, to prevent sunken graves. Call the cemetery you are considering to find out their requirements.

❑ **Decide where to buy the vault or grave liner**
It may be more convenient to buy from the funeral home; it may be less expensive to buy directly from the cemetery.

Cemeteries

If you live in the country, you might be able to have a portion of your land registered as a family cemetery. Most of us, though, are buried in existing cemeteries.

❑ **Decide what *type* of cemetery you want**
There are two types: the traditional monument cemetery, and the memorial park. In the *traditional cemetery,* you can choose any kind of headstone, monument, or grave marker. In the newer *memorial parks,* only grave markers are used and they are set flush with the ground to make it easier to mow the lawns. The memorial park cemetery may also include mausoleums.

In addition to the cemeteries run by private businesses, many communities have church, veteran's, municipal, and other nonprofit cemeteries. If you decide on a veteran's cemetery, contact your nearest Veterans Affairs office. The spouse and minor children of a vet may also be entitled to free burial in a national veterans cemetery.

❑ **Decide on the specific cemetery**
Once you have a cemetery in mind, here are some questions to ask the funeral director or cemetery manager. Does the cemetery permit headstones or require ground-level markers? Does the cemetery require grave liners or vaults? Do they sell them? What are the costs for digging and closing the grave? Is there an extra charge on weekends? How well are the grounds maintained? Is the maintenance cost annual or a one-time only fee? Does the cemetery belong to a professional organization with a Code of Ethics? And finally, consider whether you want the cemetery close to home, to make visiting easier.

❏ **Decide what kind of plot you want**
Do you want a double plot, for husband and wife? A family plot? A delicate situation arises in cases of second marriages. For instance, suppose you were previously married and bought a double plot with your first husband, who is already buried in his half of the plot. If you don't want to waste the plot, but you and your second husband would like to be buried together, you could both be buried in the remaining half of the plot. The cemetery will simply dig deeper on that side of the plot — eight feet instead of the usual six.

Is the location of the plot within the grounds important? Cemeteries generally charge more for high ground than for low ground, and more for a view. The view doesn't help your loved one, but it may be appealing to you if you plan to visit often.

Grave markers and monuments

A *marker* is a flat piece of bronze, granite, or marble to mark the gravesite. A *monument* is a freestanding piece of sculpture or stonework. If you want to put up a monument, be sure the cemetery allows that before purchasing a plot. Once you know that a marker or monument is allowed, there is no hurry to purchase it right after the death. Take your time; wait until you are less pressured.

As well, it's a good idea to let the ground settle for a while before putting up a monument so that the foundation will be firm.

❏ **Find out if there are any regulations about markers or monuments at the cemetery you have chosen**
Most cemeteries have strict regulations on the size, materials, and placement of markers and monuments. They may even have rules about the wording and length of inscriptions.

❏ **Decide what the inscription will include**
On the 12-inch by 24-inch markers common in memorial gardens, there is no room for an epitaph. If you do have room, consider ways to make this memorial truly expressive of the spirit of the one you loved. Among the items that can be included on a marker or monument are:

▸ Full name

▸ Dates of birth and death

▸ A quotation

"Here a pretty baby lies
Sung asleep with lullabies,
Pray be silent, and not stir
Th'easy earth that covers her."

— Robert Herrick, *Upon a Child*

"The woman I loved has stepped into silence;
Shut is the wood where the gods walked."

— Scharmel Iris, *The Woman I Loved*

▶ A comment
  — *He brought us love and laughter*
  — *A friend to all who knew her*
  — *His word was his bond*

▶ Artwork
  One woman, whose husband had been a dedicated fisherman, had a fishing scene carved on the monument. Many firms now use personal computers and even color printers to produce a mock-up of the artwork so you can approve it before work begins.

What to Do If You Choose Cremation

A crematory may be part of a funeral home or operated as a separate business. Once you have chosen cremation, there are other decisions: which crematory, whether or not to buy an urn or container, and how to distribute or take care of the remains.

Crematories

❑ **Decide who will do the cremation**
If you ask a funeral home to make the cremation arrangements, the funeral director may encourage you to change your mind and choose a traditional funeral with viewing and earth burial. As an alternative, some communities have firms that specialize in direct cremation. These firms support simple, no-frills dispositions. On the other hand, if you are using a funeral home to help arrange the service, it may be easier to let them organize the cremation too.

Urns

❑ **Decide whether you want an urn or container**
An urn is a small vase-like container, which is often used to hold the cremated remains. Urns come in all sizes, shapes, and materials. An urn may be made of ceramic, brass, wood, bronze, or marble. Urns that are purchased from a funeral home or cemetery office may cost from $30 to thousands.

If you want to keep the remains at home, you may want to purchase an urn. On the other hand, something handcrafted may be more meaningful: a pottery vase or jewelry chest, for instance, or a small box lovingly built by a family member.

If you plan to distribute the remains, you don't need to buy an urn. The crematory will package the remains in a sturdy cardboard box, or a tin or plastic container. For the average adult, the remains fill a box of about 12 inches by 4 inches. Rather than the box, you might bring your own container to the crematorium, when you come to collect the remains.

❏ **Decide what to do with the remains**

If the remains are to be buried, you will have many of the same decisions to make as if you were burying the body. If you have decided to use a niche in a columbarium, do you want an indoor or outdoor niche? What will you have inscribed on the front panel? Do you want a double niche or a single niche large enough for the whole family? The most expensive niches are at or near eye level. There may be additional fees for opening and closing the niche, for the name plate and for flower vases.

Ashes are sterile and nonpolluting. If you want to scatter the remains, be sure to ask the crematory to make the bone fragments small enough for distributing. Some jurisdictions have laws prohibiting the scattering of remains; others require a permit. Ask your funeral director. Also ask if there are any firms in your area that specialize in unique ways of distributing the remains, such as a plane to spread them over a mountain, or a ship to scatter them at sea.

Distributing the remains

❏ **If you will be distributing the remains, decide where to do so**
The act of scattering the remains can be traumatic for some people. Consider having an uninvolved person to take care of this.

Think of places that were especially loved by the deceased, close to home or far away. You can walk in the woods, by a favorite lake, or on the old family farm. Be sure to ask permission if you want to use private property. What about using the remains to create new life, by planting a tree? Some survivors choose to mix the remains with the soil in flower beds and rose gardens at home. Every time the roses bloom, you will be reminded of your loved one. If you make this choice, however, consider what will happen if, some day, you move away.

You might make this choice for pets, too. Our sweet old cat, Polly, is buried in the flower garden at our friend Jeannie's house, a place where Polly spent happy hours lazing in the sun.

Chapter 6 ❧

Visitation and

Viewing

This chapter may help you decide whether or not to have a visitation or viewing. The topics are

▸ About visitations

▸ Preparing for a visitation

▸ About viewings

▸ Preparing for a viewing

About Visitations

A *visitation* is when the body is laid out in the casket (which may be open or closed) before the service so that mourners may come to "visit." A visitation offers a chance for people to "pay their final respects" to the dead person. Just as important, the visitation can be a time for mourners to meet and console each other in a more informal setting than at the funeral.

You can schedule a visitation for as little as half an hour on the day of the service, or it can last for several days before the service. The visitation can be restricted to just close family and friends, or be open to the public, or a combination of both. During any part of the visitation, you can choose to leave the casket closed or open.

Is there a special ceremony?

As part of the visitation, you can arrange a formal ceremony, an informal ceremony, or none at all. The formal ceremony might be a brief service with the saying of the rosary (for Catholics) or prayers for the dead led by a mourner or member of the clergy.

The term *wake* is sometimes used to describe the reception after the funeral or memorial service. Traditionally, though, a wake means the friends and family keeping watch by the body before it is safely buried — especially through the night. (Hence the term "wake.") In some families, there is much drinking and feasting and storytelling during the vigil.

For those who are comfortable with it, an informal storytelling session can be a wonderful way to remember the person. The stories don't all have to be solemn, nor do they all have to show the person as a saint. We often love people as much for their flaws as for their strengths. Remember, too, that laughter is as much a sign of strong emotion as tears or anger. And if the person had a good sense of humor, there are bound to be some funny stories. This sharing can be a rich and powerful experience. You might even want to tape record this event to listen to again, later.

Preparing for a Visitation

If you decide to have a visitation before the service, here are some decisions to make:

❑ **Where will the visitation be held?**
Although it is usually in a funeral home, you may be able to hold the visitation in a church, a hall, or even your home (if local government regulations and your church allow this).

❑ **What date and times will the visitation be?**
If the visitation is at home, you might allow visiting around the clock, with family members keeping vigil through the night. But be careful not to exhaust yourself. You need your rest to get through the next few days.

❑ **Will the visitation be private or open to the public?**
You may not be ready yet to cope with condolences from acquaintances and strangers. If so, a private visitation is best. To compromise, set some hours aside for just the family and close friends, and leave other hours open.

❑ **Will there be a formal ceremony?**
If so, what will be included in the ceremony? Who will lead it? What time will it be?

❑ **Will there be an informal storytelling or wake?**
If so, will it be during public or private hours? Do you want someone to take the lead and manage the event?

❑ **Do you want a guest book at the visitation?**

If the visitation is held in a funeral home, the funeral director will provide a guest book, on request.

❑ **Do you want an open casket during the visitation?**

An alternative to the visitation

Because a visitation will add considerably to the costs of the death, you may want to consider a simpler alternative. Mourners can get together, informally, in someone's home before the service, without the body present. In this way, you could still have the prayer service or informal storytelling. To symbolize the person, you might bring along a favorite photograph, or some characteristic possession: a tool, toy, painting — whatever reminds you of him or her.

About Viewings

Viewing and cremation are the two topics on which there will likely be the greatest differences of opinion among family and friends. Viewing the body is enormously helpful to some; the very idea horrifies others.

Viewing means to have an open casket. In other words, the lid or the upper portion of the lid of the casket is left open so that mourners may take a last look at the deceased. Many grief counselors feel that viewing the body helps mourners to accept that death has really occurred. And once the death has been accepted, healthy grieving can begin. This may be especially important for those who had not seen the person for a while.

Your clergyperson may have his or her point of view on this question. Certainly members of your family will offer opinions. Whatever you decide, it is unlikely you will please everyone. There are no clear-cut answers, and emotions can run high. Let your guiding principle, therefore, be what you feel is right *in this situation*. The circumstances of the death, the person's age, and the feelings of other mourners may all play a role in your decision.

Following the deceased's wishes

If you are fortunate enough to know the deceased's opinions on viewing, you may want to honor those wishes. Perhaps you know, but do not agree. In that case, you may want to follow your own heart. It is best to make the decision you can live with most easily. If you do not know what the deceased wanted, listen to your own feelings. Remember that there is no "wrong" or "right" decision. You are making the best choice you can, under difficult conditions.

What happens at a viewing?

You may have a viewing as part of a visitation or as part of the service, or both. When a viewing is held as part of a service, it is usually done at the conclusion. Those mourners who wish to view the body will file slowly past the open casket. Some mourners will take only a brief glance and move on; others may stop for a moment to say a quiet goodbye. Some mourners may want to leave a flower or a memento — a favorite book, a small symbol of the person's work or play, or a souvenir of times shared together.

Keep in mind that if there is a viewing, *no one attending is under any obligation to look at or touch the body.* This is a personal decision for each of the survivors.

What will the body look like?

In most cases, the body will *not* look like the person as you remember them. Your most vivid memories may be of moments of strong emotion — times of laughter, tears, or anger. Or you may remember the liveliness of this face in conversation with you, the animated gestures, or the sound of the voice. None of that will exist, and so this person may not seem real.

Does that mean that by looking at the body you will forget how the person looked in life? For some, that is a concern. ("I want to remember him the way he looked the last time I saw him.") For most people, however, simply looking at a favorite photograph again will be enough to bring back the memories.

If the person had recently known much pain and suffering, the face will seem at peace and that may be a relief to you. If the death was sudden — from an accident or other violence — there may be even more desire for a viewing. Mourners may be overwhelmed by disbelief and denial that the death has occurred. Viewing the body may help the survivors to accept the death and begin grieving. If the face is disfigured, however, a viewing may be too upsetting. Your funeral director can advise you.

How is the body prepared?

If there is to be a viewing, the body will need to be embalmed within about eight hours after death. Although the funeral home can arrange for clothing at an additional cost, it is best to use the person's own clothing. When preparing clothing for the body, include underclothing and shoes as well. Even though only the top half of the body is usually displayed, it is a matter of dignity to clothe the whole body.

As for cosmetics, ask the funeral home to apply them with a light hand. It is distressing to see garish colors or too much makeup. For a woman, you might bring her own cosmetics to the funeral home, along with information as to how much makeup she ordinarily wore. Perhaps she always wore a certain shade of brown eye shadow, and never wore blusher. The funeral director will appreciate the use of a photograph, especially one showing how you want the person's hair arranged. Most funeral homes have a hair stylist and barber on call.

What about jewelry?

The question of whether or not to bury the person with some of their jewelry can be another difficult subject. A man may want his wife buried wearing her wedding ring. Parents may want to bury a child with the young one's birthstone. But if there are living relatives or friends who might value the jewelry, it may be better not to bury it.

- -

A DECISION NOT TO VIEW

"When an old person dies after his or her powers have declined greatly from their prime, it is helpful to the survivors to have the memory of this person redirected to the good years of his or her life. Before my father-in-law died, his mental powers had failed and life had become an unhappy burden. His death produced a mixture of grief and thankfulness accompanied by a certain amount of guilt. There was no viewing of his remains. At the memorial service we brought into focus what he was and did and stood for in the good years of his life. From that day on we carried with us the image of the fine strong person he was during those years. No amount of cosmetic restoration could have taken the place of that. In fact, any viewing at all would have detracted from the desired effect."

— Ernest Morgan, *Dealing Creatively with Death*

- -

Preparing for a Viewing

If you decide to have a viewing, here are some of the decisions you may be called upon to make:

- ▶ Where will the viewing be held?

- ▶ Will the viewing be a part of the service, or only held before, or both?

- ▶ What hours will the viewing be?

- ▶ Are there any characteristic objects you want to include with the body?

- ▶ What clothes will the body wear?

On your *To Do List* (page TK 12), add the tasks of preparing and delivering the clothes.

SAYING GOODBYE TO BRENT

Heather Carroll writes of the death of her brother, Brent, who was killed in a truck accident at age 26. Steve Baldwin, the young funeral director, was one of Brent's friends.

"When Brent's body was ready to be seen by the family first, we had to decide on what casket, what he would wear and whether we should have an open casket or not. Steve Baldwin suggested we have a closed casket with a picture, but we still had to decide for ourselves.

Even though Brent looked much older, Steve had done a beautiful job piecing his face back together. His body was so fragile we could not touch from his chest up. It was very shocking at first and very unbelievable but we felt in order to accept his death we had to see him dead and have those two days and nights to look at him whichever way he looked for the last time.

I wished myself that I had put a rosary in his casket to guard and protect him. I believe it has that power, but I didn't and deeply regretted not thinking of it at the time. My father wrote a note and inserted it in his suit pocket. No one knows what he wrote but those little actions seemed very important to us all.

My youngest brother, Steve, placed a guitar pick in his casket and Brent's girlfriend took her chain from her neck and placed it in his hands before the casket was closed. So you see there is just something about giving him a little piece of us to be with him forever, that meant so much."

— Heather Carroll, *Saint John, New Brunswick*

Chapter 7 ❦

Estimating

Your Costs

In this chapter, we look at the costs of the service and disposition. Here are the topics

- ▶ What are you buying?

- ▶ What are they selling?

- ▶ Analyzing the costs

- ▶ Some low-cost alternatives

- ▶ Preparing a budget

- ▶ A worksheet for estimating your costs

- ▶ Paying for the funeral

What Are You Buying?

Making funeral arrangements generates a complex mixture of emotions in most of us. We want the best for the one we loved, yet we may be appalled at the costs. In all states, and most Canadian provinces, funeral homes are required by law to give you a detailed price list *if you ask for it*. It may seem crass to think of money at a time like this, but not thinking about money can have dreadful financial consequences after the funeral. The bills can take years to pay off, and the survivors may have difficulty in meeting monthly expenses.

Sometimes a family will use all of the money from the life insurance or death benefits to pay for the funeral. Would it be a better memorial to the deceased to use some of this money to help those he or she loved — or indeed, to help others in the community who may be less fortunate?

Coping with guilt

In any relationship — no matter how loving — there are regrets and unresolved feelings. To cope with these feelings, we may unconsciously choose to spend a lot of money on the death ceremonies to make up, somehow, for what wasn't perfect in the relationship. But a large funeral is not proof of love and a simple service and disposition are not proof of uncaring. There are many ways to re-member someone. A costly funeral is only one.

If there was anger and misunderstanding within the relationship, you may feel guilty now. But we all feel "survivor guilt" — no matter how happy the relation-ship was. So how do you resolve that guilt? One choice is to spend less on the funeral and more on the well-being of the living. For example, you could give to a charity that the deceased supported, or that you believe in.

The value of the casket

Casket prices can range from as little as $150 for a particle-board box to $20,000 for a mahogany casket. An expensive casket, burial vault, or crypt is not a "last gift" to the deceased. The dead cannot benefit by such a gift. If such choices give comfort to you, by all means choose them. For instance, if you plan to visit the crypt often, you might want an attractive place to come to.

When you enter the selection room at the funeral home, you may see that the caskets have various warranties (for example, "guaranteed for 40 years" or "per-manent protection"). It may be a difficult thing to think about right now, but remind yourself that *no casket or burial vault or grave liner will prevent the body from eventual decay.* It does not matter how well sealed the casket or vault is, whether it is made of steel or cement or bronze, or what the warranty says. Eventually, the body will disintegrate.

If you can accept this fact, you may decide to let the body return to earth as quickly and naturally as possible. If so, cremation or burial in a simple, wooden container is a better choice than a gasketed metal casket.

. . . .

A PERSON'S WORTH IS NOT MEASURED

"In life, a person's worth is not measured by the abundance of things he possesses. In death, his worth is not to be calculated by the extravagance of his funeral or the elegance of his tombstone."
— *"Christian Burial," (booklet), The Committee on Christian Faith of the United Church of Canada*

. . . .

What Are They Selling?

The funeral industry in North America is big business. Funeral homes and related services gross $9 billion a year from 2 million funerals. In the U.S. the Funeral Rule offers good protection for buyers of merchandise and services at the time of death. One of the most important provisions is that funeral service providers are required by law to provide *itemized* price lists of all goods and services before arrangements are made. You do not need to meet face-to-face with a funeral director to receive the itemized prices. He or she is required to disclose prices over the phone, on your request. Here is an excerpt from "Consumer's Choices to Funeral Planning," a publication of the U.S. Congress, February 1986, describing the funeral rule.

· ·

SUMMARY OF THE U.S. FTC FUNERAL RULE

"The following is a summary of what the funeral provider must let the consumer know in accordance with the funeral rule. The funeral director must notify the consumer, in writing, that:
· **embalming is not required by law, and that the consumer has the right to choose direct cremation or immediate burial.** *—However, certain funeral arrangements which include viewing, may make embalming a practical necessity, and thus a required purchase. If the funeral arrangements being selected make embalming a required purchase, then the consumer must be notified ahead of time. Also, the funeral provider may not charge a fee for unauthorized embalming unless it is required by State law. For example, in most States, the funeral provider must embalm the body within a certain amount of time if refrigeration is not available. If an authorization for embalming cannot be obtained before such time as dictated by State law, then the funeral provider may charge a fee for performing this service.*

   · **it is the consumer's right to buy an unfinished wood box or alternative container for direct cremation.** *—The provider cannot claim that State or local law requires a casket for direct cremations, and must make an unfinished wood box or alternative container available for direct cremations.*

   · **there is a charge or fee for buying cash advance items.** *—Cash advance items are goods or services that are paid for by the funeral provider on behalf of the consumer. Some examples of cash advance items are flowers, obituary notices, pallbearers, and clergy honoraria. Some providers may charge the consumer their cost for these items. However, the funeral provider must disclose if a service fee is added to the price of cash advance items, or if the provider gets a refund, discount, or rebate from the supplier of any cash advance item. If the cost of cash advance items is not known at the time of purchase, the funeral provider must write down a 'good faith estimate' of their cost. The funeral rule does not require any specific form for this information. Therefore, funeral providers may include this information in any document they give the consumer at the end of the discussion about funeral arrangements.*

   · **consumers have the right to choose only the funeral goods and services they want.** *—Consumers have the right to question what is included in any line item on the statement of goods and services. For example, the term or category 'professional services' is often used as a line item cost. However, 'professional services' tends to be a general term and may include several services, almost any of which the consumer has the right to refuse. Exceptions to this requirement must be disclosed on the statement of goods and services selected and must cite the specific law that requires the purchase of any particular item.*

   In accordance with the funeral rule, funeral providers may not claim that embalming or a particular type of casket, vault, or grave liner has indefinite preservative effects on the body. Providers are also restricted from making false claims that State or local laws require vaults or liners in a cemetery."

—Chairman of the Select Committee on Aging, *House of Representatives,*
"Consumer's Choices to Funeral Planning," Comm. Pub. No. 99-541.

· ·

COSTS OF A TYPICAL FUNERAL

Costs for a funeral-home funeral vary widely throughout North America and price lists differ from firm to firm within each community. However, the following prices will give you some idea of what the charges may be if you opt for the "traditional" funeral service and burial. The prices were obtained from a variety of sources, including printed material from trade organizations. For an in-depth look at costs, see The High Cost of Dying, *an excellent 1994 book written by former funeral director, Gregory Young.*

PROFESSIONAL AND ADMINISTRATIVE SERVICES

Arrangements and Supervision by Director	$450
Recording and Registrations	$300
Embalmer's Professional Services	$275
Dressing and Casketing of the Body	$75
Funeral Home Staff (for Visitation)	$300
Funeral Home Staff (Service Day)	$250
TOTAL PROFESSIONAL AND ADMINISTRATIVE SERVICES	**$1,650**

FACILITIES AND EQUIPMENT

Preparation Room	$100
Visitation Room	$300
Reception Room	$250
Chapel or Setup in Church	$200
TOTAL FACILITIES	**$850**

TRANSPORTATION

Transfer from place of death	$95
Preparation of transportation permits	$45
Car for clergy	$80
Family Car	$80
Funeral Limousine	$150
TOTAL TRANSPORTATION	**$450**

MERCHANDISE (PURCHASED FROM THE FUNERAL HOME)

Casket (sealed, metal)	$1,700
Vault or other Outer Enclosure	$700
Guest Register	$25
Prayer Cards	$35
Acknowledgment Cards	$30
Temporary Grave Marker (while permanent marker is being prepared)	$25
TOTAL MERCHANDISE	**$2,515**

CASH DISBURSEMENTS (EXTRA COSTS PAID BY YOU OR BY THE HOME ON YOUR BEHALF)

Flowers	$250
Cemetery Plot	$400
Plot Opening and Closing	$300
Newspaper Notices/Obituary	$150
Death Certificates	$80
Burial/Cremation Permit	$3
Clergy Honorarium / Mass Offering	$125
Organist Honorarium	$50
Long distance calls / faxes	$20
Headstone or grave marker	$450
TOTAL CASH DISBURSEMENTS	**$1,828**

TOTAL CHARGES, ALL CATEGORIES (Taxes not included)	**$7,293**

Unfortunately, there is no such comprehensive legislation for consumers in Canada. However, Canadians can simply be assertive: You can refuse embalming if it is not required in your situation, ask for an alternative container for burial or cremation, ask for an itemized price list, and refuse any goods or services you do not want. If any seller of funeral or burial merchandise claims that there is legislation covering some area you disagree with, ask to see a copy of the legislation.

Analyzing the Costs

The costs listed on the previous page are representative of what is currently being charged in North America today for death services and burial. According to the National Funeral Directors Association, most funerals in the U.S. cost between $3,000 and $8,500, with the average cost in 1997 about $6,000. The cost of the burial is additional. A specific funeral home will not necessarily list the charges in this way, they may have more or fewer categories, and the actual value of the goods and services will certainly differ from one firm to the next. But the list will at least give you an idea of how many different costs there are in a typical funeral, and how quickly they add up.

The "extra costs" include all the items that are not directly related to the costs of burial or cremation. For instance, the cost of flowers, the obituary, honorariums, guest books, and so on. These costs may be listed under headings such as "cash advances" or "cash disbursements" or "stationery."

Some Low-Cost Alternatives

Here are several suggestions that may help you significantly cut costs:

1. **Rent the casket instead of buying it**
   Many funeral homes have set aside some of their top casket models in several price ranges, for rental purposes. These can be used for the service and for viewing. If the funeral director does not mention this option, simply ask. If the body is to be cremated later, it can be transferred after the service from the rental casket to a low-cost container for cremation. Be sure to take a look at the actual unit that will be used to make sure it is in good condition.

2. **Buy an inexpensive casket and then cover it completely with a heavy cloth (a pall) or a flag**
   No one attending the service need see the casket. A handmade quilt or tapestry makes a beautiful covering, especially for someone who loved crafts or needlework.

3. **Call the Memorial Society**
   To take advantage of memorial society benefits, a person must become a member before death. But even if the deceased was not a member of a memorial society, call anyway. Many local societies will provide nonmembers with information about the services available and comparative costs in your

community. If you can't find a memorial society in the phone book, call Directory Assistance.

THE BIGGEST FACTOR IN INCREASING COSTS

"By far the biggest factor in increasing funeral costs is the desire to have the casket present in the funeral home for viewing or during a service. This will incur increases in the funeral director's services and the cost of a better quality casket. In addition, embalming may be required if the casket is to be opened to the public or if it remains unburied or uncremated for a period of time. There will be facility costs and the service charges will increase."

—Gregory W. Young, *The High Cost of Dying: A Guide to Funeral Planning*

Preparing a Budget

If you have chosen a traditional funeral and costs are a concern to you, take a few moments now to prepare a budget. Using a pencil, start to fill in the budget form on the next page with some numbers.

1. **Find out how much money you have available to spend**
   Were any part of the costs prepaid by the deceased? Search for contracts with a funeral home or memorial society. See what services they cover and whether the contract has been paid in whole or in part. Do you have money available from insurance or other death benefits? Finally, see how much money is available from bank accounts.

2. **Set the maximum amount you want to spend**
   This figure should be less than the amount available; there may be some unforeseen expenses.

3. **Estimate your costs**
   Estimate the costs of the funeral, burial, and extra expenses. Make phone calls to several firms to find out the costs of the goods and services you want to purchase.

4. **Compare your estimated costs with the maximum amount you want to spend**
   If the costs exceed the maximum, find ways to cut expenses.

CASH CONTRIBUTIONS TO THE FAMILY

"Funeral expenses can be a hardship to a family that lacks finances. Cash contributions in lieu of flowers would be so helpful. I received several cash donations to funeral expenses. I was so grateful, as I was left with no assets and a heavy mortgage."

— Tillie Howe, *Yorkton, Saskatchewan*

A Worksheet for Estimating Your Costs

1. Estimate the funds available to you

Prepaid costs

Prepaid funeral costs	$_____
Prepaid vault or grave liner	$_____
Prepaid burial plot	$_____
Prepaid cremation	$_____

Funds available from death benefits

Auto club insurance	$_____
Canada Pension Plan	$_____
Employee benefits	$_____
Fraternal organization benefits	$_____
Life insurance benefits	$_____
Social Security (U.S.)	$_____
Totten Trust (U.S.)	$_____
Union benefits	$_____
Veteran's benefits	$_____
Workers' Compensation	$_____
Other death benefit funds	$_____

Funds available from other sources

Checking account	$_____
Savings account	$_____
Other funds	$_____

Total estimated funds available   **$_____**

2. Set the maximum amount you want to spend $_____

3. Estimate your costs

Funeral costs

Casket	$_____
Facilities and vehicle	$_____
Professional services	$_____
Other costs	$_____

Burial costs

Grave plot, crypt, or columbarium niche	$_____
Memorial or marker	$_____
Opening and closing the grave	$_____
Perpetual care	$_____
Vault or grave liner	$_____
Other costs	$_____

Additional expenses (not covered by funeral home contract)

Flowers	$_____
Food and drink for visitors in the home	$_____
Long distance calls or faxes	$_____
Memorial stone, including inscription	$_____
Musicians' fees	$_____
Obituary (if placed by you)	$_____
Perpetual care costs	$_____
Special requests	$_____
Thank you or Acknowledgment Notice	$_____
Other costs	$_____

TOTAL ESTIMATED COSTS   **$_____**

Paying for the funeral

When you meet with the funeral director, you will be asked to sign a contract outlining the goods and services you are purchasing for the service and disposition. At that time you will be asked how you intend to pay. Many funeral homes now take the major credit cards. Most will work out a payment plan for you, especially if there are death benefits or insurance monies coming to the estate. If you are experiencing financial hardship, let the funeral director know from the beginning. You will not be denied a dignified funeral.

Chapter 8 ❧

Meeting with the Funeral Director

If you are able to organize your own private memorial service and burial, you may not need a funeral director. For most of us, however, the funeral director plays a key role in helping us produce the formal ceremonies of death. The clearer you are about what you do and do not want, the more satisfying the ceremonies will be.

Here are this chapter's topics

▸ Choosing a funeral director

▸ Establishing a good relationship

▸ How to prepare for the meeting

▸ What to do during the meeting

Choosing a Funeral Director

If you live in a small community, you may already know your funeral director well, but in large urban centers, there is a bewildering array of firms and promises. How do you choose? Here are some suggestions.

❑ **Find out whether the deceased had already made arrangements**
Check the deceased's important papers to see if he or she had filed a pre-planning form with a funeral home or memorial society, or if there is a prepaid contract with a funeral home. This is the simplest solution: You will now know the deceased's wishes, and at least some of the arrangements will be prepaid. Of course, you can use a different funeral home, but it might take considerable time and effort to collect the prepaid funds from the first home. Check also to see if there is a prepaid deed for a cemetery plot.

❏ **Decide what your criteria are for a good funeral home**

Do you want a firm close to your home? Do you want the firm that offers the best prices? Is the personality of the funeral director important to you? (You might prefer a funeral director who seems warm and compassionate. Someone else might prefer the funeral director to be completely businesslike and not intrude upon the family's grief.) How easy is the parking? Would you like to have the reception at the same place as the service so people don't have to drive to a second location?

❏ **Check and compare several firms**

The clergy deal regularly with funeral directors, so your local minister or priest may have a recommendation. Also ask neighbors and friends in the community. You might also check the obituary pages. Is one funeral home listed far more often than the rest? That may be because it has a good reputation.

Make several phone calls before choosing a particular firm, to compare costs and approaches. If you're checking through the Yellow Pages, look at the business and professional associations each firm belongs to. This can be an indication of the firm's intention to follow good business conduct. For instance, members of the NSM (National Selected Morticians) pledge themselves to honor a "Code of Good Funeral Practice." You can pick up a copy of the code at member firms. Keep in mind that membership in organizations like the Better Business Bureau or Chamber of Commerce does not guarantee fair prices or quality services; it simply means the firm has paid membership dues to that organization.

Establishing a Good Relationship

In the relationship with a funeral director, your primary objective is to organize a service and disposition that suits you and the other survivors — both emotionally and financially. The funeral director's primary objective is to run a profitable business. Can these two positions be reconciled? Yes, if you understand how your respective roles differ.

Your role

Even if you have done a great deal of planning before the death, during the actual arranging you may be disoriented or otherwise suffering from the effects of shock and grief. You are in a stressful, and unfamiliar situation. You probably do not know the federal and state or provincial laws regulating the funeral industry, which may have a bearing on some of your choices. You are required to make on-the-spot decisions. You do not have any standards by which to judge the goods and services offered.

You may be angry at the one who has died (a common and completely natural feeling). The difficulty comes if you take that anger out on a "safe" person — the funeral director.

The funeral director's role

The funeral director, too, is operating from a complex background. He may be somewhat defensive, because of the tough scrutiny his industry has taken over the years (from Jessica Mitford's scathing 1963 book, *The American Way of Death,* to the Federal Trade Commission's more recent hard-fought investigations).

As well, the funeral director may see himself as the arbiter of the "right way" to conduct a funeral, judging those who buy a "quality" (that is, expensive) casket as more caring than others. He may even see himself as being a professional grief counselor — a role the true professionals would dispute.

At the same time, the funeral director must make a profit in order to stay in business. In many parts of North America, the field is overcrowded. The average funeral home in the United States does fewer than 100 funerals per year — about two a week. And because a small number of large firms get the majority of the business, most homes average less than one funeral a week. Yet the firm must have staff and facilities ready seven days a week, 52 weeks a year.

To determine his "average overhead per case," the funeral director will add up his operating expenses, salaries, equipment and facility costs for the year ahead. That figure divided by the number of funerals per year then becomes the lowest price at which the funeral home can break even. To make a profit, he must of course do better than that. Consequently, each funeral must bear a portion of the overhead for the days on which there are no funerals.

Guidelines for the relationship

Whatever his flaws and foibles, the funeral director is facing and dealing with death every day. His is a difficult and stressful occupation and he deserves society's gratitude. Here are some guidelines to keep in mind for a mutually workable relationship:

1. Start from the assumption that the funeral director is a businessperson and that this is a business relationship you are developing. Realize that some of his suggestions and comments about "what most people choose" may stem from a desire to sell more goods or services.

2. Treat him with respect and he will likely respond in kind. (People usually behave in ways that match our expectations of them.)

3. Listen to his ideas about what is "correct" or "the best way," but realize that these are only his opinions. The funeral director's recommendations will likely be based on convention, while you may be planning a more creative and original service — one that is more meaningful to you and the other survivors than the traditional format.

4. While maintaining respect for him as an individual and expressing gratitude for his services, *hold your own needs and wishes higher* when making all decisions.

How to Prepare for the Meeting

For most of us, the funeral home is a dreaded and daunting place. From the moment you enter the door, there is an atmosphere of heaviness and loss. For many, there is the added fear of being taken advantage of. But unlike most buyers of funeral goods and services, you have done your homework. You have made most of your decisions — and estimated your costs — ahead of time. You have come prepared, and there is no better protection than knowledge.

❏ **Collect what you need to take with you**

If you have worked your way through the material to this point in the book, you are far more knowledgeable than most survivors. Nevertheless, you probably have a number of specific questions to ask, to make your final decisions. List your questions now on the *Questions for the Funeral Director* form on page TK 10. Take with you any prepaid planning forms, contracts, or cemetery deeds. If there is to be a viewing, also bring clothing, a pair of shoes, makeup, and a recent photograph. If you want the funeral home to place the obituary for you, bring your written notes.

❏ **Take along a "guardian angel"**

When you go to the funeral home to make the arrangements, it helps to have someone with you to act as your supporter. Your clergyperson might be a good choice, especially if he or she is knowledgeable about the funeral business and supportive of your choices. Keep in mind, though, that the clergy must deal with this funeral director again; if what you want is a tough negotiator, you could be putting your clergyperson in a difficult position.

A friend or neighbor might also be a good choice. Your ideal "angel" is some-one who is assertive, has a good head for business, has experience making funeral arrangements, and is not emotionally distraught by this death.

❏ **Brief your supporter on your decisions and budget**

For your supporter to be of the most help, you must be frank about what you want and what you are prepared to pay. Show him or her the decisions you have made, and your budget. Make it clear that you are responsible for any decisions to do with the form and content of the service and disposition. Your supporter's role is to watch out for your interests, ask questions, and clarify details.

What to Do During the Meeting

Most meetings to make the arrangements take place at the funeral home. But if you would be more comfortable meeting in your own home, simply ask the funeral director to come to you.

Making the arrangements

If you have not already done so, your first task during the interview will likely be to complete three forms: one for the removal of the body from the hospital or nursing home, one for the registration of death (from which the official Death Certificate is drawn up), and finally, the burial or cremation permit.

The number of death certificates required will depend on the complexity of the estate. Ask the funeral director to estimate how many *original* death certificates will be needed. Many of the institutions that require a death certificate — government agencies, banks, insurance companies — will accept a photocopy. (Since originals of the death certificate will cost $10 or more apiece, using photocopies can be a significant saving.)

You can then let the funeral director know your decisions and requests for the service and disposition. He will help you to work out a schedule of events and to coordinate all the key participants (clergy, musicians, pall bearers, and others), and to check all the small details. If you wish, he can also help you with the obituary notice.

During the interview with the funeral director, there may be issues that you do not clearly understand. Be persistent in getting your questions answered completely. There are so many worries at a time like this; it's best to eliminate as many as you can. After the interview, you may not remember exactly what was said, so ask your supporter to take notes during the meeting on the *Questions for the Funeral Director* form. This is not rude; it is important for your peace of mind.

Selecting the casket

For me, choosing the casket for my grandmother was the toughest part of the entire funeral experience. Even though the family had agreed beforehand that a moderately priced casket would be best, in the first dark moments of being in the selection room, I felt as if I was putting a dollar value on Grandma's life, and on our love for her. Fortunately, I soon reminded myself that while Grandma liked quality things, no one had ever accused her of extravagance.

Donald Flynn, a practising funeral director for 25 years says: "The Selection Room is the profit room."

Typically, the most expensive caskets are near the entrance, with the budget options toward the back of the room. If none of the caskets displayed are in your price range, ask to see one that is. If the funeral director says something disparaging about your choice of casket or your refusal to buy a vault, either ignore the comment completely, or quietly say something like, "We choose to remember Father in other, more meaningful ways." Or find another funeral director.

It is perfectly all right to ask the funeral director to leave you and your supporter alone in the selection room. In fact, many will offer to do so. If you are tempted at this point to throw your budget out the window and buy a more expensive casket, remind yourself of your reasons for making the original choice.

Negotiating and signing the contract

Prices are generally not fixed, but open for negotiation. If you ask, you may be able to arrange for cost reductions on some services and merchandise. Ask about discounts for prepayment of the funeral, for paying with cash rather than a credit card, and special rates for seniors and veterans.

Before you sign the contract, make sure it spells out, in detail, exactly what you are paying for — and how much it will cost. Politely, but firmly, ask the funeral director to break down the costs for you, and to subtract from the total any goods or services you will not be using. This is your last opportunity to change anything about the contract you don't like or to question anything you're not sure of.

Unless you are planning to use the funeral director's help in claiming the insurance and other benefits, there is no reason to reveal any financial information. In fact, if you will be filing the claims yourself, ask for a deduction from the "professional services" charge that is an item on most funeral service price lists. At the same time, the funeral director needs assurance that he will be paid for his services. Let him know how and when you intend to pay, and bring the meeting to a close.

Chapter 9 🌿

Writing
the Obituary

In this chapter, we will look at

▶ Purposes of the obituary

▶ What to include

▶ How to place the obituary

▶ The Card of Thanks

Purposes of the Obituary

Although an obituary is optional, here are four reasons you might want to prepare one.

1. **An obituary is an announcement of the death to the community**
   Even if you are able to contact all the friends and acquaintances you know, there may also be people you do not know who would want to hear of the death.

2. **The obituary is an invitation to attend the service**
   You can include details of time and place for those who would like to come to the service but do not know how to get in touch with you or are afraid to intrude.

3. **The obituary is a permanent record**
   Many people clip and save the obituary of someone they have known, as a memento. You may have noticed that in most newspapers the obituaries are never split into two columns; if there is not enough room at the end of a

column to print the whole obituary, it begins instead at the top of the next column.

4. **An obituary can be a chance to celebrate the person's life and deeds**

   As you will see in some of the following examples, a thoughtfully written obituary can be an opportunity to pay tribute to all that was best about the person.

What to Include

If you have already gathered information for a eulogy, you have most of the information you need for the obituary. The following list includes points that can be included in an obituary. Other than the name and the date of the death, none of the items are essential and they can be in any order you like. The examples are printed in italics.

▸ **Full name**

Put the last name first. Often the maiden name or a nickname is included in parentheses.

— *GOLDBERG, Patricia Ann (Barker)*
— *SINGH, R.J. (Rob)*

· ·

A GRAND OLD LADY

"BROWN — Henrietta Beatrice (Bea Pascoe) died quietly at the kitchen table just after breakfast . . . at the grand age of 92 and with her marvellous sense of humor still intact. Bea will go back to her beloved farm at Boharm, Saskatchewan. Bea saw tremendous changes in her lifetime but never veered from a most wonderful outlook on everything that happened around her.

She had a great memory, especially of poetry and would quote at the slightest chance. One of her favorites was 'Sea Fever' by John Masefield. She probably would have quoted these lines: 'And all I ask is a merry yarn / From a laughing fellow rover, / And a quiet sleep / And a sweet dream / When the long trip's over.'

And finally, hockey has lost one of its greatest fans. There will be no service, but a reception to celebrate Bea's life will be held at the Langhouts' on Saturday . . ."

— *Obituary for Henrietta Brown*

· ·

▸ **Age**

▸ **Date and place of death**
   — *Died in Chicago on December 3.*
   — *On the first of May, at home in Green Lake.*

▸ **Cause or description of death**
   — *Passed away quietly on (date).*
   — *At peace after a long illness.*

— After a courageous fight.
— Died suddenly on (date).
— Died in her sleep.
— Died tragically on (date).
— Went peacefully to be with her Lord.
— Andre died after a very valiant fight for life. In his 8 months, he brought much joy to his grieving parents.

▸ **Date and place of birth**
— Born August 18, 1963, in San Diego.
— Born 89 years ago in Glasgow, Scotland.

▸ **"Predeceased by"**
Traditionally, the names of those in the immediate family who died before the deceased are given before the names of the survivors. The names most commonly included are those of the spouse, children, parents, and sometimes brothers and sisters.

Sometimes the person will be predeceased by a first spouse; it is perfectly correct to list that person here, even when there is a living second spouse. A situation such as this can be delicate, however. Consider the feelings of the living spouse when making this decision. If possible, talk about it first with those involved.

— Predeceased by her loving husband, Albert.
— Predeceased by her first husband, Walter Kozak, in 1974.
— Carla is now reunited with her husband, Charles, who passed away on (date).

▸ **"Survived by"**
When there is a surviving spouse, that person's name should be first (although if the couple were divorced, and the divorce was not friendly, you may want to omit the spouse's name). Sometimes the surviving children are listed next; sometimes the parents or brothers and sisters. Each of the people in the immediate family is usually listed by name and sometimes by place of residence.

If the person was involved in a close relationship or had a special friend, it is thoughtful to include their names too.

It is generous to include the names of all those who cared deeply for the person, even though the relationships among the survivors are complex. An obituary for one 18-year-old boy included among his survivors his mother, stepfather, adoptive father and natural father.

— He is sadly missed by Marie, his loving wife of 46 years.
— Mourned by his dear companion, Charles Lee.
— Will be missed by his many friends, especially the seniors at Cloverdale Pentecostal Church.

▶ **Occupation, career, or accomplishments**

An obituary can include professional achievements, such as starting a business, or long service with the same company, special interests — anything that characterized the person. Think about business achievements, community service, honors and awards, number of years lived in the community, and so on.

> — *Raminder was a farmer all his life. He loved the land and he passed that love on to his five children.*
> — *Erma was a long-time member of the United Church Women's Auxiliary.*
> — *David's dedication to his patients and the principles of clinical medicine won him the respect of his patients and colleagues, and his conduct as a general practitioner exemplified the highest and best ideals of this branch of medicine.*
> — *Consuela was a founding director of the Multicultural Society, working ceaselessly to promote racial and religious harmony. Her interest in the welfare of the general community remained to the very end.*
> — *Bernice excelled as a mother, grandmother, and dear sister.*

▶ **Education**

You might want to mention post-secondary degrees or awards for educational achievement.

▶ **Military service**

You could include the branch of the services the person belonged to, important action seen, and any medals or honors.

> — *Al served overseas in the Second World War.*
> — *Dennis was a devoted, lifetime member of the American Legion.*

▶ **Memberships**

If you wish, include clubs, church groups, hobbies, sports, political associations, unions, and/or volunteer work.

> — *Mr. McElhinney is a Past President of F.O.E. #20.*
> — *Margaret was also well known in figure skating circles, being a team member of the North American Champions from 1932 to 1938.*

▶ **Thanks**

You may want to thank specific doctors or nurses, clergy, devoted friends, or helpful organizations.

> — *All are grateful to the staff at Evergreen House for their loving care.*
> — *We thank that magnificent group of rare human beings who perform miracles in the Palliative Care Unit. You looked after the whole family.*

▶ **A message from the deceased, prepared before they died**
> — *Joshuah wanted to thank his many friends for their love and support during his illness. Special thanks to . . .*

▶ **Personal notes**

— She is also survived by her special friends, many of whom called her "Grams." Particular affection was in her heart for her long-time friend and physician, Dr. John Boswell and those friends and nurses who helped make her last days the best possible. She lived a long full life, rich in love and understanding. She died surrounded by those who loved her and will be sorely missed by all of us.

— Walter's courage during his suffering was an inspiration to all who knew him.

— Her warmth and wit made her days with us very special. A great lady who will long be remembered.

— Her family and wide circle of friends came to admire her determination and fortitude in the face of so many physical assaults upon her person over the years. Right to the end, Jennifer maintained that spark of wit and fine character we all came to respect and admire. She will not be forgotten.

▶ **Date, time and place of service(s)**

You could include any or all of the following: prayer service, viewing hours, funeral Mass or service, memorial service, graveside ceremony, reception, or wake. If there is to be no service, it is a good idea to let people know that.

You might want to include the exact address of the funeral home, including where to park (if parking is difficult in the area).

— No service will be held, at Cecil's request.

— The family will receive guests at home from 11 a.m. to 1 p.m. on June 1st.

— Following Mass, friends are invited to join the family for refreshments at the Parish hall.

— A party, as requested by Bill, will take place on Saturday at 2 pm at the Golf Club. The family looks forward to celebrating Bill's life with all his friends and acquaintances at that time.

▶ **Name of priest, minister, or rabbi**

— With Rev. John Hennessey officiating.

▶ **Burial place or notice of cremation**

— Interment at Parkview Cemetery.

— Cremation, by request.

▶ **Flowers or memorial**

A phrase like "in lieu of flowers . . ." is a serious bone of contention with many florists. In some areas, they have successfully lobbied newspapers to keep the phrase out of obituaries. If you want to suggest a memorial donation, it can be to a favorite charity, or to assist research of the disease the person died of.

— Flowers gratefully declined. Donations to the Cancer Fund appreciated.

— If desired, donations may be made to the Alzheimer Society or Multiple Sclerosis Research in Frederick's name.

— At Monica's request, no flowers.

— *A donation to the Elks Club Children's Fund (in memory of her grandson Alfred) would be appreciated.*

. . . .

"COURAGEOUS FAMILY MAKES PLEA FOR OTHERS

DEAR ANN: I just read an obituary that knocked me out. Not because the death was tragic, but because the family was willing to publicize the awful truth and plead for the sake of others.

I am 70 and scan this section every day. I doubt that many people under 30 read the obituaries, but everyone reads Ann Landers. I hope you will print this. — A Seattle Devotee.

Dear Seattle: That obituary is a testimony to the courage of Debbie's family. So far I've received 37 copies. Yours was the first. Thanks for sending it on.

DEBORAH ELIZABETH HAGGERTY

Born June 22, 1959 in Seattle, died Feb. 17, 1988, of cardiac arrest due to cocaine abuse. She was a beautiful young woman with strawberry blond curls, a gentle soul and a generous heart. She loved music and backgammon and all growing things, especially roses. She was a gifted writer whose work, known only to a few, showed insight and sensitivity. She died a victim of poverty and drugs — each undermining her ability to fight the other.

The lesson of her life is this: If you know someone who is hurting, reach out to that person today; if you are hurting yourself, ask for help. Debbie leaves behind a grieving family: her mother, Mary; her brothers, John, Michael and Gregory; her sisters, Cassandra, Pamela, Linda and Marilee; six nephews and nieces; her partner, Michael, and numerous friends."

— Ann Landers' column, *Chicago Tribune*

. . . .

How to Place the Obituary

Usually, you can deliver the obituary notice personally to the newspaper or read it over the phone. If you are having trouble with the words, the classified operators or your funeral director will be able to help you. In most places, the newspaper will charge you for the obituary notice and the cost can easily reach several hundred dollars. You can place it yourself or have the funeral home do so.

Place the notice for as many days as you want, either before or after the service. Most notices appear for only one or two days.

. . . .

HAVING THE LAST WORD

"The classified gal asked if I realized how much the notice would cost. I told her that it was being paid for by the estate and it was my final dirty trick on Mom, who was quite well fixed in her final years, but never learned how to spend money on anything she considered 'not essential.' As I walked out of the press building, I smiled to myself, looked skyward and said 'Gotcha!' "

— Bob Clarke, *Victoria, British Columbia*

. . . .

You may want to include a favorite photograph of the person or the symbol of his lodge or fraternal order or the Legion, if he or she was a member. (The newspaper may already have these available.) Including the symbol allows other members who are scanning the obituary page to see quickly that one of their own has died.

If the person was well-known in the community, you might also want to notify the editorial department of the newspaper, and the local radio and television stations. They may want to run a news story on the death.

Did the person grow up in another town or spend many years in another community? Consider placing a notice in the old hometown paper as well.

The Card of Thanks

As an alternative to the obituary — or in addition to it — you might want to place a Card of Thanks in the newspaper. This notice can be used to recognize the efforts of hospital staff, family, and friends — in short, anyone who helped during the crisis of death and dying.

. . . .

A THANK YOU

"We, the parents and brother of Andrea Joy Rogers, who was taken from us so tragically in the hit-and-run accident of May 25th on Doran Rd, wish to thank all of the people who came to her assistance. The person who found her on the road, the person who called the ambulance and the ambulance staff. The staff of the Lions Gate Hospital, especially Elaine Henders and Dr. Mayo. Her dear hometown friend, Greg MacDougall, who received support from Shelly Fedigan, Donald McInnes and Frank Von Possel during the long vigil with Andrea before she finally gave up the fight. Her fine friends in Vancouver who so fittingly held a memorial service and planted a tree in Headwater Park.

We are striving to purchase an electric wheel chair for Lynn Valley House in Andrea's memory and would appreciate any donations. Andrea gave of herself in her short life and we are comforted to know that others did the same for her in her hour of need.

— Sincerely, Mr. & Mrs. Ralph Rogers & Craig"

. . . .

TONI'S OBITUARY

"ALAIN, Toni Theresa (Simpson) died gently in her sleep Tuesday morning, safe at home beside her beloved Phil and dear sons Shawn and Jamie. Treasured and loved by Mum and Dad, Fay and Duncan Simpson; big sister, Sheila and Bob Martin. Deeply loved and missed by her second family, Grandma Irene Alain; Roger and Anna Alain; Noella, Rocky, Lisa, John and Amber MacDougall; Carmen, Chris, Krista and David Grant; Marc, Doreen, Nicole and Christopher Alain; and by so many friends and family.

Although she often thought of herself as shy, over the years Toni blossomed into a woman of great courage and strength — a leader for us all in our search for inner peace. She delighted in flowers, especially irises and roses; she had a devotion to and talked often with the Virgin Mary; angels were her friends. We hope you're enjoying those new wings of yours, Toni. We love you with all our hearts.

Instead of flowers, the family suggests donations for a stained glass window at St. Luke's in Toni's honour, or a gift to Operation Eyesight Universal."

. . . .

THE STRENGTH OF LOVE

Love is as strong as death.

— Solomon

Chapter 10 ❧

The Day
of the Service

In this chapter, we look at this important day in three stages

▶ Before the service

▶ During the service

▶ Following the service

Before the Service

By this time, most people are running on nervous energy. Even if you are suffering from exhaustion and lack of sleep, you may still be unable to slow down and relax. Here are some practical suggestions for preparing yourself, both physically and emotionally, for the day ahead.

Preparing yourself physically

If you have guests staying with you, it's a good idea to organize a bathroom schedule. Make sure everyone has time for a bath or shower, and that there is enough hot water for everyone. If you think there might not be, send a guest or two to a neighbor's house. Encourage your guests to use their bedrooms, rather than the bathroom, to do hair and put on makeup.

Leave more time than usual to dress and do your hair. You may be interrupted many times by phone calls or last-minute details to take care of. You will certainly be more distracted than usual.

Choose comfortable shoes. You may be on your feet for a long time today, talking with other mourners before the service and at the reception.

A few more suggestions:

❑ If your eyes are swollen from crying or lack of sleep, dab some witch hazel onto a tissue or cotton ball and apply gently around your eyes to reduce the swelling.

❑ Pack some tissues or handkerchiefs in your pocket or purse.

❑ Put checks or cash for the honorariums into sealed envelopes and pack them in an inside jacket pocket or purse.

❑ Take a camera if you would like photographs of the casket, flowers, or friends and family attending the service.

❑ Be sure there is enough gas in all the cars that will be used today.

❑ Before you leave, check the stove, iron, and appliances to make sure everything is turned off.

Preparing yourself emotionally

Have some quiet time before you leave for the service. Ask the others in the house to be silent, too, or even to leave you alone for a few moments. Now put on some gentle music — perhaps light classical or new age music. Sit down in a comfortable chair with a glass of juice or cup of tea.

Close your eyes and pay attention to your breathing for a moment. Now rehearse in your mind what will happen today. See yourself greeting friends and family before the service, listening to the eulogy, hearing the music. Listen to the minister saying a few prayers at the graveside. Feel yourself shaking hands and embracing people at the reception.

See yourself behaving in exactly the way that is right for you — whether that be a dignified calmness, or spontaneous tears, or even laughter in some moments. Speak a few silent words to your loved one, perhaps a private goodbye. Now take a deep breath and move out into the day.

. . . .

OVERWHELMING GRIEF

"I felt a sharp chest pain. I felt lactic acid build in my calves, making it hard to walk. I still don't know to this day how something didn't snap. I didn't know why or how a human being could endure such overwhelming grief."

— Michael Arthur Whitehouse, *in "Centering," Spring 1994*

. . . .

Last-minute tasks

If the reception is to be held at a church hall or somewhere outside your home, the details can be taken care of for you. If the reception is to be held in your home, check these last-minute tasks:

❏ **Prepare the food and make coffee**
Put together all the food that can be made ahead of time. Cut up dessert squares, make sandwiches, and so on. Add water and ground coffee to the urn so that it is ready to plug in.

❏ **Set the table**
Set out the serving dishes, cups and saucers, plates, utensils, and napkins.

❏ **Talk to the housesitter**
Leave instructions for the housesitter. For example: "Plug in the coffeemaker at 11:30. Take the desserts out of the fridge and slice them just before noon."

A schedule can be useful

If there is much to do, draw up a schedule or "To Do" list and tape it to the fridge. Use the form called *Day of the Service* on page TK 3. Here's an example.

8:30 - 10:00	Jean and Margaret prepare food for reception. Prepare salad greens and dressing. Slice turkey. Prepare casserole.
9:30	George: Take Aunt Rachel to hairdresser.
10:00	Minister will arrive to pick up notes for eulogy.
10:30	Alice arrives to look after house, set table, etc.
10:45	Everyone leaves for service at Baptist Church
12:30	Graveside ceremony at Mountain View Cemetery
1:00	Alice: Plug in coffee urn, please.
1:30	Guests arrive for reception here. Gone by 5?
8:15	Richard: Drive Aunt Rachel and Uncle Paul to airport.

Sometimes when we watch a person coping with the immediate aftermath of death, we say, "She's handling it so well" or "He's being so strong." In fact, that person may be like a powder keg about to go off. This was my own experience.

When Grandma died, I was the one to take over most of the funeral arrangements. Since I take pride in my organizational skills, it seemed a natural task for me to take on. As well, it felt like the best way for me to express my love for Grandma. The rest of the family were supportive and appreciative as I drew up lists, made the phone calls, chose the casket, and so on. I felt strong and strangely energized.

The morning of my grandmother's funeral, I got into my car to make the 30-minute drive to my parents' house, where we would all be gathering. As I put the key into the ignition, I was struck by a searing pain in my gut. Suddenly it seemed as if the whole inside of my body was in spasm, twisting and turning me inside out. Almost doubled over, I eased my way out of the car and back up to the apartment — not even remembering to close the car door behind me, so great was the pain.

I called my family to say I wasn't sure if I could make the funeral. My cousin, Rod, volunteered to come and get me. But gradually, over the next half hour, the pain subsided and I was able to drive home. The experience dramatically showed me, however, that those who seem most in control are the ones in greatest danger of collapsing under the stress.

— Sheila

During the Service

For many people, the first funeral service they attend in their adult life is one for someone in the immediate family. The unfamiliarity of the event can add to your stress. Services can be vastly different from each other: A Catholic funeral Mass in a New York City cathedral will be nothing like a rural Quaker memorial service. What all services have in common is the desire to pay tribute to the one who has died and to give mutual support to the mourners.

Funeral etiquette

If there is a guest book, it will be at the back of the church or hall for everyone to sign. The immediate family usually sits in the front pews. You can choose to be seated as soon as you arrive or to stay in the back to greet other mourners.

If the casket is to be present during the service, the funeral director will organize the pall bearers to lift the casket out of the funeral car. They may carry it all the way to the front of the church, or simply lift it onto a cart, which will be wheeled to the front of the room. The funeral director will show the pall bearers what to do and where to sit.

The minister or other presider will announce the opening of the service and will introduce each new event in the ceremony. If there is to be a viewing at the end of the service, the funeral director will then open the lid of the casket (usually only the top half of the lid). Mourners may now view the body — stopping for a few moments, or simply filing past. When the service is over, the funeral director will close the casket and will lead the pall bearers in returning the body to the hearse. The family will leave their seats, followed by other mourners, starting at the front of the church, row by row.

Coping with your emotions

Tears and other signs of emotions are a healthy and natural expression of grief, for both men and women. However, if you want to calm yourself at any time, focus on your breathing for a few moments . . . breathing in peace, breathing out pain. If other thoughts intrude, return your attention to your breathing until you are quiet again.

After the Service

Following the service, people will gather in little groups in the back of the church or hall, perhaps hoping to exchange a few words with you. Stay to talk if you are up to it and have the time. Otherwise, just nod your thanks to well-wishers as you make your way to the car.

Distributing honorariums and flowers

If the funeral director is not taking care of the honorariums for you, now is the time to distribute them to the professionals involved in the service. Simply offer the person the envelope and say something like, "Thank you, pastor. I appreciated your kind words about Lee" or "Thank you for the organ music, Mrs. Brown. It was lovely."

You must also let the person in charge know what is to be done with the flowers after the service. If there are weddings or christenings coming up in the church where the service was held, you may want to leave them. Flowers may also go to the burial site, to shut-ins in your community, to hospitals, or home with you.

If you do take flowers to the grave and want photos of them, be sure to take them that day. A friend of my mother's returned the day after her husband's funeral only to find that all the beautiful bouquets had been stolen.

What to expect at the grave site

If there is to be a service at the grave, the mourners will now get into their cars and follow the hearse to the cemetery. At the burial site, the minister or other presider will wait until everyone is gathered around the grave and then will begin the brief committal ceremony. At the end, one or more people may want to throw a flower or a handful of dirt into the grave.

What to expect at the reception

The reception is another opportunity for mourners to offer you their sympathies. Some may be people you do not know. If you don't want to talk, simply say, "Thank you so much for coming" and move on. You may want to keep busy, looking after coffee and refreshments, or you may want to let others take over. You may want to sit down in a quiet corner, or you may feel a need to keep circulating.

As with everything else in the death experience, there is no right or wrong way to behave at the reception. Whatever feels fitting to you is right.

After everyone leaves

When the last guest has gone, get into your most comfortable clothes or a favorite robe, so you can begin to wind down. If you still have overnight visitors and you need some time alone, take yourself away for a long relaxing bath or a quiet drink.

After all the noise and confusion of this day, try to have as little stimulation as you can tonight. Some quiet conversation or recounting the events of the day with other family members can be helpful.

· ·

A MAN'S DYING

"A man's dying is more the survivor's affair than his own."

—Thomas Mann, *The Magic Mountain*

· ·

Chapter 11 🌱

Practical Matters

The service is over. The commotion has died down. Your visitors have left. You may feel completely numb. Or perhaps you feel searing physical pain, starting from your heart. You are probably exhausted. You simply cannot face all the tasks you know must be done. None of it seems important anymore.

Don't rush yourself. Take all the time you need. Know that you are doing the very best you can at each moment. When you are ready, there are a few practical matters to be looked after, including

‣ Writing to friends and family

‣ Sorting through belongings

‣ Organizing the household

Writing to Friends and Family

You may be writing to notify friends and family of the death, or to thank them for kind words or deeds.

Check the *People to Notify Later* list (page TK 8) and *Gifts Received* (page TK 5) for the names of people to write to. If you have the energy, you may want to write thank-you notes even to people you have already thanked in person — neighbors and family. They will appreciate your taking the time to formally acknowledge their support.

Preparing to write

Most of us put off writing letters at the best of times. How much more difficult it is to write letters after a death. One way to make it easier is to prepare a working area first, a space that is comfortable and easy to work in. The idea is to create a place where you can settle down and write immediately, whenever it is convenient or the mood strikes.

Do you want to keep a copy of the letters you are writing? If so, and you are handwriting or typing, use carbon paper. If you use a computer, print a second copy. You might also want to include a photocopy of the obituary or the program from the service.

One letter at a time

Perhaps you feel you can't get started, yet the project is looming over you like a dark cloud. Set a timer for 15 minutes, sit down and simply address a few envelopes. Once the timer goes, you may find you are able to do a few more. If not, try another 15 minutes tomorrow. Even that much is an accomplishment.

When all the envelopes are ready, start with some easy letters, such as the printed death notice to be sent to people you do not know well. If you still find it difficult to tackle the main letters, ask someone to help you. Perhaps your helper can physically write some of the letters, or maybe you just need someone to sit quietly with you while you write. If someone else is writing for you, they might begin something like this: "Mother has asked me to thank you from the bottom of her heart for your kind words and the beautiful flowers at the time of Dad's death."

There is no need to come up with a completely different letter for each reply. You can draft a few paragraphs about the death or about your feelings and re-use it in all the letters. Then add a personal note to each letter.

If you have a typewriter or a computer, why not use it? It will help you get through this difficult task more quickly. Handwriting every letter is not important. What is important is to express your thanks to those who have helped. Use the computer, if you have one, to create the basic letter, changing the name, address, and salutation of each letter. You can add a handwritten second page or "P.S." to thank people personally for their specific kindnesses.

Don't feel you need to get all the letters written right away. Perhaps you can tackle only one or two letters now. That's fine. But if it starts to feel like a heavy weight on your shoulders, ask for help. It will add tremendously to your stress to leave them undone for too long.

. . . .

LEARNING HOW TO ACCEPT HELP FROM OTHERS

"People like me in the 'helping professions' find it very difficult to accept help. I am used to giving encouragement and understanding, but it has been hard for me to let others derive the same good feelings by helping me. I realize this is a selfish thing. I suppose I always need to feel in command. I am now learning to 'lean' but still to keep my independence and to do for myself as much as possible."

— Ramona Brewer, *Rossville, Georgia*

. . . .

Sorting Through Belongings

One of the most painful after-death tasks is to sort through the person's clothes and belongings. Everyone handles this differently. Some mourners will keep the person's room exactly as it was on the day of death, not touching or changing anything. The room becomes almost a shrine.

At the other extreme, there are those who immediately clear out everything — determined not to be sentimental — hiding or getting rid of every photograph, every reminder of the one they have lost.

Most of us take a more moderate path. It may be weeks before we can face the job of going through the person's things. But eventually we will do it, giving or throwing away that which is no longer of use, and keeping the things we value. It is not "morbid" as some people say, to keep photographs or special belongings on display to remind you of the good times.

What are the fears we face when carrying out this task? First, there is the simple taboo of prying into another's personal belongings. Too, we may fear that we will discover dreadful secrets. Most of all, there is the overwhelming sadness that by taking these steps we are admitting to ourselves and to the world that this person is never coming back.

When we went through Grandma's things, my aunt Lois, sister Toni and I had a few tears, but also a few laughs (for instance, at the holey long-johns Grandma had saved, probably for decades). But for Mom, it was all still too painful, and after a little while she quietly disappeared upstairs.

Making use of clothes and personal things

Belongings will be scattered throughout every room of the house, not just the bedroom. To give you a sense of accomplishment, you may want to start with the easiest places first (such as the living room or bathroom) and then move on to the rooms that remind you more strongly of the person (the sewing room, tool shed, or bedroom).

Before getting down to work, collect four big boxes and label them "To Keep," "Charity," "To Give Away," and "Garbage." Try to handle each item only once. Pick it up, make a decision about it, and place it in the appropriate box.

A few people like to work quietly on their own. For most of us, however, this is a good time to ask someone close to you for help. As you go through these things, each one will trigger memories — some good, some painful. You may want to talk about your memories and feelings to a sympathetic listener as you work. Eat something before you begin. You will need all your strength for this job.

YOUR OWN WAY OF GRIEVING

"DEAR ANN: This is for "Out West," the girl who was concerned about her mother because she keeps her deceased husband's shirt under her pillow. Each of us has his or her own way of coping with a personal loss. Far be it from me to tell somebody that his or her way is not normal.

Speaking from my own experience, I miss my brother more than words can say. When the pain becomes unbearable, I go to my closet where several of his shirts are hanging, and I pull one out and savor all of the wonderful smells. This may seem morbid to others, but to me it is miraculously thera-peutic. Please, Ann, tell that girl to leave her mother alone. Keeping her husband's shirt under her pillow might give her the greatest peace she can find at this difficult time in her life.

— EAST GRAND FORKS, MINN.

DEAR MINN.: I heard from many readers who have been down the same road. Read on:

FROM MOODY, TEXAS: Our son was born four months premature and died shortly after birth. He was the second child we had lost this way, and my husband and I were devastated.

I found it very comforting to sleep with a little kimono we received as a baby gift. When my arms ached with emptiness, I would cradle that precious garment, and it made me feel as if I still had a little part of him. I sometimes slept with it next to me on my pillow, and it absorbed a lot of tears those first few weeks. Eventually, I was able to fold it up and put it away with a little kiss.

Friends and relatives need to realize that there is no 'right' way to grieve. It's an up-and-down process that can last for several years. What is needed is nonjudgmental, loving acceptance of what-ever stage we are in. Ann, please tell your readers not to be afraid to talk about the person who died. It is comforting to know that others remember, too."

— Ann Landers' column, Chicago Tribune

Unless you have many helpers and a limited time in which to complete the work, it is unlikely you will complete this task quickly. Try to do it in chunks large enough to give you a sense of accomplishment. If all you can manage is one drawer, complete that one drawer in this session (rather than doing part of several drawers). Then reward yourself for whatever you've achieved, with a hot bath, for instance, or a walk, or some special treat.

Before you give or throw anything away, let those who were close to the person have a chance, if possible, to choose what they want. They may select things you couldn't have imagined.

If there are young children or grandchildren who are not old enough to choose something to remember the person by, you might select something that will in later years have value or meaning to the child: Grand-dad's old football jacket that a young boy can grow into, Mommy's rose silk dress for a girl.

Eyeglasses can help others

A wonderful thing to do with old eyeglasses is to donate them to be used in overseas medical missions and hospitals. In Canada, send the eyeglasses to Operation Eyesight Universal, 4 Parkdale Crescent NW, Calgary Alberta T2N 3T8 (phone 403-283-6323). In the United States: New Eyes for the

Needy, Box 332, 549 Millburn Avenue, Short Hills, NJ 07078 (phone 201-376-4093).

· ·

SOMETHING TO REMEMBER HIM BY

"My husband's clothes would not fit any family member, so that was no problem and Goodwill benefited. He would have liked that. But he had three hats that he had worn fishing. Strangely enough, my daughters and granddaughter wanted them, so I think the offer must be made regardless of what a spouse thinks personally."

— Maureen Butt, *Victoria, British Columbia*

· ·

THE GRANDMA AND GRANDPA ROOM

"My parents both died early last year, within 10 weeks of each other, and it is still hard to believe they are not here any longer. My husband and I have a four-bedroom home, so I emptied one of the bedrooms (my daughters were delighted to get all the goodies) and I have filled it and decorated it with things that belonged to my parents and grandparents (such as my grandparents' bedroom set, the folks' chair, pictures on the wall, etc.). When we walk into that room, it's like going into their home. It's great and my daughter made a beautiful sign for the door that says, 'The Grandma and Grandpa Room.' I have mother's old folding wooden clothes rack where I have placed different towels, aprons and laces that she had done. On the bed is linen that she crocheted, lace edgings, quilts and the old chenille bedspread. It truly is a room filled with beautiful memories, and has been very therapeutic for me."

— Elizabeth Kummeth, *Goshen, Indiana*

· ·

Organizing the Household

If your spouse has died, you will have the added burden of taking on all of his or her responsibilities in the life and home you used to share. Your new double role can be daunting. Take a look at the following list to see areas you may have to take on. Then think about ways to get them done. Not everything needs to be done by you. Perhaps you could hire a student or a senior to help with housework, meals, or yard work. Even young children can take on new responsibilities, especially if you have a family meeting to explain the importance of their contribution.

Keep in mind, too, that not everything that used to be done needs to be done now. Realize it can't all be accomplished exactly as it was when your spouse was there to help you.

If you are responsible now for an aging parent whose spouse has died, don't try to take on all the chores yourself. Now is the time to investigate social services (such as the Homemaker's Service available in many communities). Ask your doctor or community information referral service for help in finding support.

Daily or weekly tasks

No matter what you are going through, some chores have to be performed day after day. The routine can even be welcome, because it temporarily distracts you from your grief. In a traditional marriage, the wife will have taken care of all the housework. After her death, the husband is often at a loss to know what to do. Here is a list of typical daily tasks to be taken care of:

▶ **Cook meals**
Now more than ever, it is important to eat regular, nutritious meals. If you don't feel like eating, much less cooking, at least try to snack on things like fresh fruits, raw vegetables, and grain-rich breads.

▶ **Feed and exercise pets**
Even if you are not the one who usually takes the dog for a walk, consider doing so now. It will be a quiet time for you, but most important, you'll be getting the fresh air and exercise that will help you cope better, and sleep better. And stroking your pets can even lower your blood pressure.

▶ **Prepare lunches**
Whether or not they have done so before, school-age children can learn to make their own lunches.

▶ **Make beds**
If bed-making is a real chore for you, buy a duvet. It only takes a moment to straighten and voila! The bed is made.

▶ **Cleaning and tidying**
For most people, clutter produces anxiety, while tidiness is restful. Since one of the things you need most at the moment is peace, it's a good idea to minimize clutter. On the other hand, don't set impossible standards for yourself. If you need to, get help with heavier chores like vacuuming and cleaning bathrooms.

▶ **Shop for food and household supplies**
At first, you may find yourself buying too much food, or buying things that were favorites of the deceased. Just do the best you can, one day at a time.

▶ **Do laundry and ironing**

. . . .

WHO AM I NOW?

"One aspect of bereavement that I had not anticipated was the loss of identity. With Elizabeth gone, I was no longer me! After forty years of sharing on such a broad spectrum of life, I did not have a separate identity. . . . I understand this is more often experienced by men, while women may feel a stronger sense of being deserted."

—Ernest Morgan, *Dealing Creatively with Death*

. . . .

Outside projects

If you received offers of help from friends and neighbors, call on them now to look after some of these outside errands and chores. But don't rely on them forever. Think of this as an opportunity to share and then to learn independence.

▸ Mow lawn

▸ Do gardening

▸ Service car (regular oil and lube, tune-up, repairs)

▸ Wash car

▸ Make and keep doctor and dentist appointments

▸ Take pets to vet

▸ Buy clothes (for self and others in the family)

▸ Buy gifts (birthday, Christmas, special occasions)

▸ Take clothes to cleaners

Inside projects

During the first year or so of grieving, some people, seemingly filled with energy, throw themselves into countless cleaning and renovating projects. Others withdraw completely from all but the most essential chores, putting their energy into inner work. Each of us is unique, and we experience each death differently from any other death. Once again, you must follow your own piper.

▸ Wash and wax floors

▸ Polish furniture

▸ Clean walls and woodwork

▸ Wash windows, inside and out

▸ Defrost and clean refrigerator or freezer

▸ Clean closets and drawers

▸ Clean basement

▸ Clean garage or tool shed

- Clean fireplace and chimney

- Clean carpets

- Polish silver

- Mend clothes

"Office" work

If your spouse was always the financial manager or social director of the family, you will have to adopt a new role. Do ask for help if you need it.

- Read and answer mail

- Balance checkbook

- Pay bills

- Prepare budget or financial plan

- Prepare income tax return

- Renew insurance

- Make social arrangements

- Wrap and deliver gifts

. . . .

LIVING ALONE

"Because I had been used to having my husband here all the time it had not been necessary to remember to turn off hot plates or lock doors. This now became a problem and I made a list of what I must do and used it for several months, until those things became automatic.

Some things I wish I had known were: When is the chimney due to be cleaned? How often should I clean the furnace filters and what are the instructions? This is a renovated house and I would have liked a plan of all the wiring etc. The garden was his department and I would have liked information on his most precious plants. How to shut off the water to the outside, and where the main shut-off is for electricity."

— Maureen Butt, *Victoria, British Columbia*

. . . .

Chapter 12 🦎

Financial and
Legal Matters

Read this chapter to learn how to wind up the financial and legal affairs of the deceased and settle the estate. Here are the topics

▶ Getting started

▶ Seeking professional advice

▶ Collecting cash and benefits

▶ Probate step 1: Applying for probate

▶ Probate step 2: Paying the bills and taxes

▶ Probate step 3: Dividing the assets

The handling of wills and estates comes under the authority of the state and provincial governments. Procedures and requirements differ for each jurisdiction. The information in this chapter is not meant to be legal advice in any way. It will, however, give you an overview of what is involved. *Please consult a legal professional in your own jurisdiction.*

For those living in Washington, Oregon, British Columbia, Alberta, Saskatchewan, Manitoba, or Ontario, Self-Counsel Press publishes excellent do-it-yourself guides to settling an estate. Most of us, though, call on a lawyer to help us through the legal maze.

Your own role and duties will depend on several factors: your relationship to the one who died; whether or not there is a will; whether or not you are an executor; whether or not the will goes to probate; whether or not you use a lawyer; and how simple or complex the legal and financial affairs are. As always, just use the information here that applies to you, and ignore the rest.

Getting Started

For most of us, it is enough of a challenge to deal with our own financial affairs. How much more intimidating it can seem to sort out someone else's money matters. Yet going through this process can be a way of feeling close, once again, to the person you have lost. And there is the satisfaction of knowing that you are carrying out his or her wishes. Here is how to get started.

❏ **Check the safety deposit box**

Procedures differ from place to place, but this is what typically happens: If you are the surviving spouse or have power of attorney, a bank official will go through the box with you or your lawyer; a bank clerk will take an inventory of the contents. If there is a copy of the will in the box, you may take that right away. You may also be able to take the marriage certificate, deed to the house, insurance policies, and other important legal documents. If there is no surviving spouse, or if the estate is substantial, the contents may be "frozen" (unavailable to you) until the court recognizes the executor or appoints an administrator.

❏ **Find the most recent will**

Be sure the will you have is the *last* will and testament. Even if you have a will in your hands, the deceased may have made a new one later. If you have not found a will but believe that one was drawn up, see if your state or province has a Wills Registry. They can do a wills search, which may take several weeks. You may also come across a document called a Letter of Instruction or an Estate Record. This document often lists funeral service preferences, the location of the will, and names the executor.

❏ **Obtain certified copies of the death certificate**

If you have not already done so, order copies of the death certificate. You will need a copy for each claim you file. Not every institution needs an original; many will take photocopies. Phone or write each place to find out.

❏ **Find all the important papers**

Go through all the likely places where important papers and records might be stored. Check the obvious spots, such as desk drawers and filing cabinets. Then check places like the stationery drawer in the kitchen or buffet cupboard, the basket on the counter that holds unpaid bills, wallets and purses, the glove compartment of the car, in the workshop, the den, even in coat and jacket pockets.

Look over the following list to see which papers you might need.

▸ Bank records

▸ Bills

▸ Birth certificate of the deceased and minor (underage) children

▸ Business ownership or partnership papers

- Credit cards

- Insurance records (policies, payment stubs)

- Loan agreements (both owing and owed to the deceased)

- House and property records (land titles, assessment notices, mortgages, records of rental properties)

- Marriage certificate

- Military discharge papers

- Pension records (agreements, payment stubs)

- Safety deposit box (location, keys)

- Savings bonds

- Social Security (in Canada: Social Insurance) numbers for the deceased, spouse, and minor children

- Stocks and bonds (certificates, name of broker)

- Tax records (old returns, current receipts)

- Vehicle titles and registration

- Will

❑ **Organize the documents**
If the deceased did not have his or her papers organized, set up a file folder for each type of document. Once each document is in a file folder, go back and sort them into order by date. Now skim the papers quickly so you know where to look for any particular item — the tax records, the bank statements, the insurance policies, and so on.

❑ **Call or write the financial institution holding a mortgage on the deceased's home or holding other outstanding loans**
If the debt was covered by mortgage or credit insurance, the balance will be paid off automatically by the death of the principal.

❑ **Apply to the post office to redirect the deceased's mail to the executor**
Of course, if you are the executor and are living at the deceased's address, you don't need to redirect the mail.

❑ **Cancel medical coverage**
If the deceased was paying for his or her own medical insurance, there may be a refund for prepaid coverage. This will go to the estate. If you and the children were covered by the same plan, make sure you are still covered or that you get a new plan.

❑ **Cancel charge accounts and credit cards**
Write or phone all credit suppliers, and ask for the final statement to be sent to you as soon as possible. You may be required to return the credit cards to the companies that issued them, along with a letter announcing the death of the cardholder.

❑ **Cancel subscriptions and memberships**
Look through the deceased's checkbook for the last year to track down payments to magazines, clubs, and associations.

❑ **Take photographs of what you want to remember**
For instance, if a child's room is to be dismantled, or the old family home is to be sold, take pictures first so you'll always be able to remember it as it was.

Seeking Professional Advice

As the documents, bills and decisions pile up, you may feel alone and lost on a financial sea. On the other hand, you may be deluged with unsolicited advice. If you don't feel experienced enough to evaluate the options yourself, think about seeking professional help. If you ask for help from a close friend or relative who is a professional financial advisor, agree before you start whether you will be paying regular rates or receiving free advice.

❑ **Decide what you can do yourself and where you'll need help**
If you are a skilled financial manager and familiar with legal jargon, you may decide to take on all these tasks alone. Conversely, if you have never balanced a checkbook, your best bet is to get help with everything. If you are confident about bill-paying, for instance, but there is also a portfolio of stocks and bonds to be managed, call for professional help with the securities.

If you don't know any financial advisors, ask for recommendations from anyone you know who is likely to have such contacts — your bank manager, employer, doctor, a neighbor who has settled her husband's estate.

You may want to use the services of the funeral director or an insurance broker to collect the insurance and other claims. They are familiar with the paperwork and procedures. But find out what you are paying for this service — before you start.

If you decide to use a lawyer to handle the settling of the estate, do as much as you can ahead of time. This has two benefits: you keep the costs down, and you will be more knowledgeable about the decisions being made.

. . . .

YOU CAN NEGOTIATE WITH YOUR LAWYER

"A friend made such a helpful suggestion to me when my husband was killed that I have tried to pass the word along to others.

Lawyers can accept as low a fee as they want to in handling your affairs after such a loss. It is wise to talk to lawyers and find one that is not charging you the maximum amount. In my case I got sufficient death certificates and did the work of assembling all information. However, negotiate with the lawyer before giving him or her the case. You will be surprised. My fee was less than $200 for an estate of about $150,000."

— Evelyn F. Hubbard, *Signal Mountain, Tennessee*

. . . .

More advice

The advice you will hear again and again from the professionals is: Don't make any hasty decisions. Here is some more sound advice.

1. **Always get a second or third opinion**
   Each advisor speaks from his own perspective. The attorney will have one viewpoint; the accountant, another; the financial planner, a third. Your final decisions can be a blend of the best of this advice.

2. **Take someone with you**
   If you are still shaky from this death, you are probably not yet able to really hear — let alone remember — all that is being said to you. Ask a cool-headed companion to come with you to meetings with advisors. Her job will be to take notes, ask questions, and review the options with you after the meeting.

3. **Stay liquid**
   To stay liquid means to keep your money easily accessible. If you don't need the cash from the insurance policies right away, let it sit. If you receive money from the estate, don't use it right away to pay off the mortgage or to invest in long-term savings certificates. Keep your financial options open and you will feel much freer and more flexible.

4. **Stay put**
   Well-meaning friends may encourage you to sell the house, or move to a new place, to "get away from all those memories." If you can afford to stay, and it feels right to you, don't move for at least a year. You may need those memories right now and moving creates tremendous upheaval and stress.

Collecting Cash and Benefits

Benefits that the deceased would have received upon retirement are often available to the survivors. Check especially Social Security (in the United States), Canada Pension, life insurance, annuities, veterans benefits, and pension plans. Most benefits do not come to you automatically. You must apply for them. This includes payments from government programs. Eligibility requirements and the amounts are always changing, so it is best to check for yourself.

Before collecting money in person from banks, insurance companies, or other agencies, phone their offices. They will tell you what documents to bring and what other information they must supply. Some insurance companies require that the policy be returned to them. Before surrendering the document, photocopy the pages that describe the policy's benefits. Keep a record of your activities: contact names, actions taken, follow-up required, and so on. Use the form *Collecting Cash and Benefits* (page TK 2) to record the current status of each of your claims. Here are the most common sources of cash and benefits.

❑ **Bank accounts**

Call, write, or visit each bank or other financial institution (credit union, trust company, or savings and loan) in which the deceased had an account. Generally, if you had what is called the "right of survivorship," you can continue to draw money from the joint checking account or even withdraw the full amount. (Note that not all joint accounts have the right of survivorship.) To have a joint account transferred to your name, present a copy of the death certificate to the bank.

If checks come addressed to the deceased, take them to the bank with a death certificate and a copy of the will to prove that you are the executor. After that, you should be allowed to sign the checks, and the bank will notarize them and deposit them in the account.

❑ **Bank loan**

If you need money to tide you over until the insurance or pension funds arrive, take photocopies of the policies and other documents to the bank or other financial institution and ask for a temporary loan.

❑ **Business ownership**

If the deceased was the sole owner or a partner in a business, there may be income due from the business interests. You will need professional legal and tax advice to determine and value any business assets and liabilities. You may also have to decide whether to sell out your interest in the business, or to stay on as a partner or shareholder.

❑ **Canada Pension Plan (Income Security Program)**

The government-run Canada Pension Plan's Income Security Program gives a lump sum death benefit if the deceased contributed to the Canada Pension Plan for a minimum of three years. If the deceased was already receiving

Canada Pension benefits, this lump sum would be approximately six times the amount of the present monthly benefit.

The Income Security Program also provides a benefit to the surviving spouse, and orphans' benefits. When you apply for benefits, take along the death, marriage, and birth certificates. Also take the Social Insurance numbers for the deceased, yourself, and any dependent children. Apply to the local Canada Pension office.

❏ Compassionate Travel Refunds

Most North American airlines offer partial refunds on airfare for members of the immediate family (as defined by the airline) who are traveling due to a death. Typically, you must complete a Compassionate Travel Refund application form within 90 days of the date of the bereavement and include a copy of the Death Certificate.

❏ Group benefits (Company, fraternal orders, professional associations, unions)

Check for employee benefits. The company where the deceased worked may have a pension or profit-sharing plan. There may be a survivor's death benefit or group life insurance benefit. If you don't hear from the company, call the human resources office.

Fraternal orders and professional groups (for example, teachers) often have group insurance plans. As well, many unions have health, welfare, and pension programs that provide benefits to the survivors of members who died. Ask a co-worker or call the local union office for information. So many benefits go unclaimed because the families do not seek them out.

❏ Insurance

Insurance is often the largest source of specific benefits for spouses and children. If an insurance policy specifically names you as the beneficiary (rather than just the estate), that money can be paid immediately, often within a few days, once you have the death certificate. If no living beneficiary is named, all amounts are frozen until after probate or administration of the estate.

There are various kinds of policies to look for, starting with life, health, accident, and disability insurance. If the death was by a motor vehicle accident, there may be benefits to cover the funeral expenses and for the survivors. If the death happened on vacation, look for a travel insurance policy.

You will likely have to submit two forms: the claimant's statement and a doctor's statement. To process the claim, the insurance company will want a death certificate or copy, plus the original policy. Photocopy the policy before handing it over to the company.

❏ Loans owed to the deceased

Find out if any money — either personal or business loans — was owed to the deceased, including shareholder's advances to a self-owned company.

❑ **Savings plans and bonds**

United States: U.S. Savings Bonds in your possession that name you as the beneficiary can be cashed at any bank upon proof of the purchaser's death (a certified copy of the death certificate). Also, check to see whether the deceased had an IRA (Individual Retirement Account) set up at a bank or savings association, or a Keogh Plan (retirement plan for self-employed persons).

Canada: Canada Savings Bonds can be cashed at any bank upon presentation of a death certificate. Money in a Registered Retirement Savings Plan (RRSP) that names you as the beneficiary can be cashed within a few days after you show the bank the death certificate.

❑ **Social Security**

In the United States, Social Security provides a lump-sum benefit, which is payable to the eligible surviving spouse, or entitled children. A dependent grandchild or dependent parent may also be eligible for benefits. These benefits are not automatic; you must apply for them. Contact any Social Security office. If excluded from Social Security, you may be covered by other government programs.

❑ **Stocks**

Call the deceased's stockbroker to find out the current status of any stocks and investments.

❑ **Veteran's benefits**

United States: Regulations and qualifications for benefits are changing, so check for up-to-date information. You may be able to receive funeral expense benefits, a U.S. flag for the casket of a veteran, and a government headstone. In certain cases, there may also be funds for the surviving spouse and children. If certain requirements are met, the body can be interred without charge in a U.S. National Cemetery. Contact a local V.A. office or write to the Department of Veterans Affairs, Washington, DC 20420 and ask for the booklet, "Federal Benefits for Veterans and Dependents." On the Internet, you can check the Department of Veterans Affairs Home Page (http://www.va.gov/VA.htm).

Canada: A veteran with overseas service may qualify for a full or partial burial allowance under the Department of Veterans Affairs and the Last Post Fund. If your husband was a war disability pensioner, you are eligible for a widow's pension, and a lump sum toward funeral expenses. You will need to show your marriage certificate, your birth certificate, and the death certificate. It is helpful to know your spouse's regimental number. The Department of Veterans Affairs will continue this disability pension for one year and then provide a widow's pension. This pension does not need to be declared on your income tax return. Visit the local Department of Veterans Affairs office for information on eligibility and amounts paid. Other possible sources of benefits are the Department of National Defense and the Last Post Fund.

❑ **Wages owing**
Call the deceased's employer and ask for the wages owing at the time of death, including any holiday pay.

❑ **Workers' Compensation**
Certain benefits may be available if the cause of death is related to the deceased's employment. Laws and regulations vary.

Probate Step 1: Applying for Probate

Probate is the process of legally proving before the courts that a particular will is the genuine Last Will and Testament of the deceased. Granting of probate does not mean that the will has been declared valid: Those named and not named as beneficiaries may still challenge the legal validity of the will for a specific period of time (set out in legislation) after probate is granted.

The *estate* includes all the real property (land and buildings) and personal possessions of the deceased — in short, all the assets and liabilities belonging to the person at the time of death. This can include checking and savings accounts and securities that are owned jointly, and business holdings. Life insurance benefits to living beneficiaries are not subject to the probate process.

An *executor* (if female, the executrix) is a personal representative of the deceased, as appointed in a will. The executor has the authority to take temporary legal ownership and possession of all the deceased's assets, to buy and sell property and possessions, and to divide up the estate among the beneficiaries.

The executor is ruled by what is called *fiduciary duty,* the responsibility to act in good faith and with the interests of the beneficiaries in mind as he or she conducts the business of the estate. In most cases, the executor is entitled to a fee for his or her time and trouble.

If no valid will is found, or if for some reason there is no executor, or he or she is unwilling or unable to act, the court will appoint an *administrator* (administratix, if female) to take over the role of executor. In general, the powers and duties of the administrator are the same as those of an executor. However, since the administrator is directly accountable to the court, rather than to the beneficiaries, there is usually extra paperwork, more expense, and greater delays before the estate is finally distributed.

Not every estate must be probated. If you and your deceased spouse jointly owned all assets (such as real estate, bank accounts, pensions, and insurance), the assets can probably be transferred directly to you, without probate. If the value of the estate is less than a certain sum (as defined in your state or provincial legislation), probate is not required. Take the will to the local Probate Court as soon as possible. Most provinces and states have regulations limiting the length of time the will is valid.

For the rest of this chapter, I will assume that you are the executor. Keep all the documents related to probate together: the will, will-search document, death certificates, and the many legal forms you will fill out and sign during probate. Make a copy of every letter you write and every form you complete. Before actually filing the documents for probate, there are a number of actions you must take, beginning here.

Preliminary actions

❏ **Call or write any beneficiaries of the will**
   Often there is a reading of the will shortly after the funeral or memorial service. Whether or not there is a reading, as the executor you have the responsibility of contacting each person named in the will to tell them what bequest they are to receive and that you are applying for probate.

❏ **Safeguard any valuable property**
   If there are any valuables — such as furs, jewels, important collections, or fine art — decide how to store them safely until they can be sold or distributed. Also see that they are properly insured. If the deceased's possessions are already insured under a homeowner's or tenant's policy, notify the insurance agent of the deceased's death and ask that your name, as executor, be added to the policy.

❏ **Advertise for creditors**
   It's a good idea to advertise in the local newspaper for any creditors who might have a claim against the estate. If you do not advertise, the beneficiaries may be able to hold you personally liable for any successful claim.

Preparing an inventory

Before applying for probate, you must also prepare a complete inventory of the assets and liabilities of the estate. Depending on the complexity of the estate and your own experience, the task of calculating the estate's worth can be weighty and time-consuming. First, for every asset belonging to the estate, you must determine its value, as of the date of death. (See below.) Then list and calculate the liabilities. Combine the two sets of figures on one statement to determine the net worth of the estate.

❏ **List and value all assets**
   Make a list of all the assets you uncovered as you collected cash and benefits. Include cash from all banks and financial institutions, insurance policies, savings bonds, retirement income, pensions, stocks, business interests, and any money owed to the deceased. Now list all household goods and furnishings, and all personal possessions, including vehicles, jewelry, and other valuables. To get current market values, especially for collections and fine art, you may have to call on independent appraisers. Enter each amount in your statement of assets and liabilities.

❑ **List all outstanding expenses and liabilities**
From the documents and information you have already obtained, make a list of all outstanding expenses: service and disposition expenses, medical bills, credit card and charge accounts, utility bills, loans, and so on. Enter these amounts on your statement of assets and liabilities.

❑ **Prepare a financial statement**
Combine the information on assets and liabilities in one financial statement that details the estate's net worth.

Filing the documents

❑ **Fill out the documents required for application for probate or administration of the estate**
In most cases, you will need to apply to the courts for documents that will legally allow you to take control of the deceased's assets before you can transfer property and distribute the estate. Your application for probate will include the estate's financial statement, and a number of sworn statements that declare your right to act as the executor, your good intentions, and your declaration that you have notified all potential beneficiaries and heirs.

❑ **Transfer ownership titles into your name**
As soon as you have received approval of your probate application from the courts, transfer the legal title and ownership of all property and vehicles into your name, as executor. You are then able to use these assets either to pay debts, to transfer legal title again to the beneficiaries, or to sell them and distribute the proceeds.

. . . .

THE FAMILY AUCTION

"I don't remember whose idea it was, but it was decided to have a family auction after the funeral and then you could bid on all those items important to you and the proceeds would go to the estate. Brilliant idea. We elected an auctioneer and a secretary to keep track of who bought what. We were able to remove our purchased goods from the house when we wished and were free to let the rest of the estate go through probate at the lawyers. It solved a lot of problems for a large family especially where there was not a lot to divide. The auction was a lot of fun and many wounds were healed with good will towards brothers and sisters."

— Penny Wahl, *Regina, Saskatchewan*

. . . .

Probate Step 2: Paying the Bills and Taxes

Legislation in your jurisdiction will outline in what order the debts and expenses of the estate must be paid before the balance of the estate can be distributed to the beneficiaries. In general, though, the priority is as follows:

❑ **Pay the funeral expenses**

The law requires that reasonable funeral expenses be paid out of the assets of the estate even before claims such as administration costs, taxes, and the claims of the beneficiaries.

❑ **Pay legal and accounting fees to do with the administration of the estate**

These administration fees include, for example, the costs of probating the estate, insuring or storing the assets, couriers and communication costs for business conducted on behalf of the estate, and bills from a lawyer or accountant.

❑ **Reimburse yourself for reasonable out-of-pocket expenses**

As the executor, you are entitled to compensation for any expenses you incurred while carrying out the business of the estate. If applicable in your jurisdiction, you may also be able to pay yourself a small percentage of the estate as an executor's fee.

❑ **File the final personal income tax returns**

Check the old returns to find out the last year filed. File an income tax return on behalf of the estate for the year of the death and for any former years not yet filed by the deceased according to the requirements in your jurisdiction.

❑ **Pay any outstanding medical bills**

Under some health insurance plans, any outstanding hospital or doctors' bills are automatically paid after death, provided the premiums for the months in which the services were rendered are fully paid. Check with the insurer.

❑ **Pay any other outstanding debts**

Now you must pay all the rest of the debts and obligations you listed on the statement of assets and liabilities. The executor or administrator may be held personally liable for these debts if a valid creditor remains unpaid after the distribution of the estate.

❑ **Collect any outstanding debts owed to the estate**

❑ **Sell assets from the estate**

If there is not enough cash available in the estate to take care of the debts and expenses, you must convert other assets into cash. For instance, you could sell vehicles or stocks, cash in savings bonds, or sell jewelry. Sell personal items first to meet expenses, before using cash legacies or property that is part of a bequest.

❑ **Pay estate and inheritance taxes**

In some locations and in certain circumstances, the estate will be liable for the Federal Estate Tax or Inheritance Tax. Most people would be wise to seek help from an attorney or financial advisor before filing these returns.

Probate Step 3: Dividing the Assets

As executor, you are accountable to the beneficiaries for the safeguarding of the assets and for every financial transaction you make. Be sure you have detailed and accurate accounting records, supported by bills and receipts, for every step you take.

When distributing the assets to heirs and beneficiaries, it is a good idea to get a signed release from each person, acknowledging receipt of the gift and agreeing to give up any future claims against the estate.

❑ **Distribute specific monetary and property bequests according to instructions in the will**
If there is not enough cash to pay any cash legacies, sell or redeem other assets from the residue of the estate.

❑ **Distribute the residue of the estate**
Whatever is left in the estate now is to be distributed to the beneficiaries or heirs according to the provisions of the will and/or the applicable law.

SMALL THINGS

"We cannot do great things. We can only do small things with great love."

—Mother Teresa

Chapter 13 🌿

Your Own

Planning

Read this chapter to learn about

▶ Making your will

▶ A living will or healthcare directive

▶ Considering organ donation

▶ Considering bequeathal

▶ Considering memorial societies

▶ Planning your own arrangements

▶ Holding a family conference

▶ Organizing the paperwork

▶ Alberta's Expected Home Death Program

For low-cost legal assistance in drawing up your will or a healthcare directive, or recording your preferences for your own final arrangements, see the section called "Legal Expense Plans" on page 157.

Making Your Will

A *will* is a written legal document, made during your lifetime, which contains your wishes for estate disposal, and takes effect upon your death. A will has four key purposes:

1. Your will determines how the assets of your estate are divided up. An estate is made up of property (land and buildings), money, jewelry, and other personal possessions.

2. Your will names and appoints one or more executors, who are responsible for settling the affairs of your estate and carrying out the instructions in your will.

3. If you have dependent minor children, your will allows you to appoint their legal guardian, who will be responsible for their upbringing and education.

4. Having a will may reduce taxes to be paid on your estate.

Even if you have a small estate, it is expensive and inconvenient for your survivors if you die without leaving a will. The court will have to appoint an administrator to take over the duties that would have been performed by your executor. This will likely mean delays in the processing of your estate, which could result in unnecessary financial hardship for your family. Not having a will also means that a percentage of your estate will go to lawyers and the courts — money that could have gone to your heirs.

Should you draw up your own will? If you choose to do so, there are various self-help publications that include sample forms of wills, available at many bookstores and stationery stores. There is even computer software available to guide you through drafting a will. But given the importance of this document and the impact it will have on those left behind, I truly feel it is best to see a lawyer. For a simple will, you can expect to pay a lawyer perhaps five hundred dollars or more. This outlay, however, could end up saving your estate thousands of dollars in administration costs.

In general, a will must be dated and signed by you and two witnesses, to be legally valid. If you move from one state or province to another, have your will checked by a lawyer in your new home. Wills are governed by state or provincial laws, and there is no uniformity between them. For instance, a handwritten will is valid in some jurisdictions, but not in others.

You may also include, in the will, your instructions about funeral arrangements and disposition, but these instructions are not legally binding on your executor. In any case, a will is not the place to record your wishes about your funeral or organ donation or the like. That information should be given to your next of kin while you are alive, or kept where it can be found immediately upon your death.

Preparing to draft the will

Before making an appointment with a lawyer, prepare yourself by doing the following:

❏ **Decide who to appoint as your executor**
Be sure to ask the person you are considering if he or she agrees. Being an executor can be a time-consuming and stressful responsibility. It is not to be given or undertaken lightly.

❑ **Decide who is to be the guardian of your underage children**
Since the guardian will be responsible for your children's health, education, and upbringing, be sure you have purchased enough life insurance or established a trust fund to give the guardian adequate financial resources for this responsibility.

❑ **Give instructions for the care of your pets**
If you have preferences as to who should look after your pets and wish to set aside money for their care, make that known here.

❑ **List all your assets**
Draw up a summary of your cash and bank accounts, insurance policies, stocks and bonds, pension plans, money owed to you, and other sources of present or future income, or death benefits. Include property, vehicles, and businesses you have a financial interest in. Also make a list of personal belongings with sentimental value that you specifically want to bequeath to a relative or friend.

❑ **List all your liabilities**
Draw up a summary of any loans you owe, mortgages, or promissory notes, including the amounts owed and to whom.

❑ **Decide how to divide up your estate**
If you wish to leave specific sums of money or real estate or articles of personal property to particular individuals, list them first. Then decide how the balance of your estate is to be divided.

❑ **Decide where to store the will**
The worst place to store your will is in your safety deposit box or locked in a safe; it may be difficult to get to after your death. The best place is probably in your lawyer's office. Keep a copy at home and consider giving a copy to other important people in your life. In any case, let other people know where the will is.

A Living Will or Healthcare Directive

If you were ill with no chance of recovery and couldn't speak for yourself, who would speak for you? The *Living Will* (also known as a healthcare directive) is a document that enables individuals, while competent, to inform family members and health-care providers of their wishes about the use of life-sustaining treatment when death is imminent.

For instance, one clause in the Living Will prepared by the organization called Choice in Dying states: "I, _____, being of sound mind, make this statement as a directive to be followed if I become permanently unable to participate in decisions regarding my medical care. These instructions reflect my firm and settled commitment to decline medical treatment under the circumstances indicated below . . . ." The instructions continue: "However, I do want maximum pain relief, even if it may hasten my death."

A 1993 Gallup poll showed that although 75 percent of U.S. adults say they approve of living wills, only 25 percent have prepared one. Choice in Dying, a New York City-based nonprofit educational organization, constantly monitors the legislation in each U.S. state. Any U.S. citizen can get a free, preprinted living will form, appropriate for their state, and a guide to completing the form by calling 1-800-980-WILL. Canadians can get information and forms from the University of Toronto web site *www.utoronto.ca/jcb/living_wills.htm*

A signed, dated, and witnessed Living Will is recognized by the courts in many jurisdictions. Such a document can help family members and physicians to make difficult decisions which often arise in the last days or weeks of life.

. . . .

THE VALUE OF A PREPAID SERVICE

"I am really thankful that we had used a prepaid funeral service. Not that the prepaying was needed in my case, but the information that they required was a real value. In my shock, I did not remember all that we had discussed. That really surprises me because I am a very down-to-earth woman and I did not think I would be so emotional. So I highly recommend that even if such a plan is not used that the information they require is written down and signed."

— Maureen Butt, *Victoria, British Columbia*

. . . .

Considering Organ Donation

In Chapter 2, "Taking Care of the Body," we discussed the decision to donate the organs of the deceased. Here, we look at making the decision about donating your own organs. (Recent studies have found that a higher percentage of us are willing to agree to donating someone else's organs than are willing to donate our own.)

Be part of a miracle

Every day tens of thousands of North Americans wait anxiously for new organs and tissues. In November 1998, for example, there were 59,808 people awaiting transplants in the U.S. Your decision to become an organ donor could mean the chance for a dramatically improved quality of life — or even the gift of life itself — to someone else. In your own state or province, there are people waiting for organ and tissue transplants, including eyes, kidneys, heart, lungs, liver, skin tissue, bones, and pancreas. As many as 12 recipients, in transplant centers across the continent, can benefit from the organs from one healthy donor.

Only about two percent of deaths occur in a way that allows solid-organ dona-tion. Typical donors are victims of aneurysm (which can cause fatal bleeding in the brain), motor-vehicle accidents, drownings, suffocation, and cardiac arrest —

situations in which the heart can be artificially supported after brain death occurs.

A common fear for a potential organ donor is that the hospital's treatment of you will not be as aggressive as for other patients. In fact, the doctors who care for critically ill patients and who are responsible for declaring brain death are different from the doctors involved in organ retrieval and transplant operations. The only concern of the hospital staff is to save your life.

The surgical techniques used on an organ donor are the same as those used in an operation on a living person. The body is treated with respect. A few hours after the operation, the body is returned to the family and all funeral arrangements — including viewing — can proceed.

Most representatives of the major religions support the idea of organ donation, as a meaningful way of helping others. If you need reassurance about your church's position, talk to your clergyperson before committing yourself as a donor. If you change your mind later, you can withdraw from the program by tearing up the donor card or removing your name from the registry.

How to become a donor

1. **Find out about your local organ donor program**
   Most organ donor and transplant programs are run by the provincial or state government. If you can't find the program in the phone book, try a community information referral service or ask a local hospital, doctor, or nurse.

2. **Sign a Uniform Organ Donor card and carry it in your wallet**
   This card is legal authority for donation in Canada and the United States. Even if you are registered as an organ donor on your driver's license, it's a good idea to carry an organ donor card in your wallet or purse as well. In some jurisdictions, an organ donor decal is placed on your medical CareCard.

3. **Talk to your family about your wishes**
   Even though a signed donor card is a legal document in most jurisdictions, in practise, the medical institution will almost always ask permission from the immediate family before proceeding.

   You don't want your family to be startled by a request for your organs at the time of your death, so talk to them about it now. This has two benefits. First, it is more likely that your wishes will be carried out when the time comes. Second, it gives you a chance to reassure any family members who may be uneasy about organ donation of its value and importance to you.

4. **Talk to your doctor**
   Your doctor may be less than enthusiastic about your plans. Medical doctors — trained to save people — sometimes feel that death is a failure, rather than

a natural and necessary part of all life. For these reasons, doctors are not always eager to talk about organ donation. In fact, doctors are much less likely than the rest of the population to become organ donors themselves.

Find a quiet moment to let your doctor know that you are donating your organs, and that his or her help would be appreciated, should the circumstances arise.

Considering Bequeathal

Bequeathal means donating your entire body for use by a medical school to help train doctors and dentists, or to be used in medical research. A practical advantage of bequeathal is that you avoid most or all of the customary funeral and burial expenses. Although most medical schools will eventually return the ashes to the family (if requested), all schools do have the facilities to take care of disposition themselves.

How to arrange bequeathal

To plan for a bequeathal, follow these four steps:

1. **Call your nearest medical school for a bequeathal certificate**
   If you don't know the name or phone number of a nearby medical school, call your doctor, the local memorial society, or the local hospital.

2. **Talk to your family about your wishes**
   Even though most jurisdictions recognize that you have legal control of your own body, discussing this matter with your family demonstrates your respect for their feelings and the seriousness of your intention.

3. **Distribute copies of the bequeathal certificate**
   Mail one copy of the bequeathal certificate back to the medical school and keep one for your own records. You might also give a copy of the certificate to your spouse, executor, doctor, memorial society, or funeral director.

4. **Make alternative arrangements**
   A bequeathal certificate does not guarantee that the medical institution will accept the body at the time of death. A body may be disqualified because of disease, systemic infection, or autopsy, for instance. If one of your objectives in making the bequeathal is economy, the services offered through a memorial society may be your best alternative.

Considering Memorial Societies

The Memorial Society is a nonprofit, nonsectarian organization of over a million laypeople, active in about 200 cities in North America. The society's purpose is "to assure dignity, simplicity, and economy in funeral arrangements, through advance planning."

These goals are achieved by the members acting together as a large consumer group to negotiate reduced prices with selected local funeral homes. The society then signs a contract with one or more firms, guaranteeing members a lower price on certain services. In most branches of the society, the work is done by unpaid volunteers, although in the larger branches there is sometimes a paid manager.

The society states that members commonly achieve savings of 50 to 75 percent over conventional funeral costs. These savings come in part through the collective bargaining power of the societies, and in part because society members usually choose simpler arrangements (for example, no viewing, and a memorial service followed by cremation).

Who joins memorial societies? According to Ernest Morgan, author of *Dealing Creatively with Death,* "By and large it has been prosperous, educated, middle-class families that have organized memorial societies — doctors, lawyers, teachers, business people. Mostly they have been church people, too, and mainly concerned with simplicity. Ironically, working-class families and minority ethnic groups, on whom the burden of funeral costs falls most heavily, have been less inclined to join memorial societies."

Morgan goes on to say: "Memorial society leaders have been concerned with this and have kept the doors of membership open to all. Some societies actively seek members and leadership from minority groups and the less affluent, with modest success in recent years."

How to join a Memorial Society

1. Pay a lifetime membership fee (usually $10 to $30). Some local societies have a small annual renewal fee.

2. Fill out a Designation Form, listing your preferences for the service and disposition, plus vital statistics for the death certificate.

3. Send a copy of the Designation Form to the nearest funeral home that is under contract to the Memorial Society, where it will be kept on file. Keep another copy for your own records and to share with your next of kin.

4. At the time of death, your survivors simply call the funeral home and tell the funeral director that you were a Memorial Society member.

If you move, your membership is transferable among all societies in Canada and the United States for little or no charge. Be aware that not every organization that has the words "memorial" or "society" in its name is actually a Memorial

Society; some are actually private companies. If you are in doubt, ask whether the society is a member of the Continental Association of Funeral and Memorial Societies or the Memorial Society Association of Canada. (See "Resources" at the end of this book for addresses.)

Planning Your Own Arrangements

When you first think about it, planning your own arrangements seems like tempting fate. As Stephen Leacock once said, "A man called on me the other day with the idea of insuring my life. Now I detest life insurance agents; they always argue that I shall some day die, which is not so."

If you can move beyond the fear of your own mortality, making your own arrangements is a most generous gift to your family. Your survivors will be spared many painful decisions, and they will have the comfort of knowing they are doing exactly what you wanted done. Here's how to plan your own arrangements.

❑ **Design your own ideal service and disposition**
Review chapter 4 through 7 of this book, and write down everything that you would like done (or not done) in your own service or disposition arrangements. You might even want to survey local funeral homes for their current prices and then specify an upper price limit.

❑ **Add the touches that will make this celebration uniquely yours**
After you have made note of the basic instructions (type of service, burial plot information, and so on), give some thought to any special requests you have that will give your own service the sound and flavor of you. Do you have some of your own poetry you would like to be read? Or a letter you've written to be read to your survivors? Do you want your golfing trophies to appear on a memorial table? Would you like your granddaughter to sing? Maybe the ushers could hand each mourner a white rose from your garden as they leave the church, or a jar of your homemade preserves.

❑ **Make an annual appointment with yourself to review all decisions**
Check over your plans once a year to keep them current. Set a date you can easily remember: New Year's Day or your own birthday, for instance, or even the anniversary of the death of a family member — a positive way to mark that difficult day.

❑ **Carry your instructions in your passport**
Each year about 9,000 North Americans of all ages die in foreign countries. Be sure to carry in your passport a note giving the exact location of your will and the names and phone numbers of your executors.

Holding a Family Conference

What about holding a family conference to discuss everyone's wishes and plans? You'll probably find that the hardest part of holding the conference is to actually set a date. In my own family, I'd been vaguely suggesting such a meeting for months. The responses from family members ranged from lukewarm agreement to horrified groans.

Gradually, everyone got used to the idea and we finally set the date: Father's Day. We had a list of tough issues to be discussed — burial vs cremation, organ donation, and so on. Then everyone shared their wildest fantasies about what a celebration of their own life would be like. When it was all over, we all felt safer, somehow, and experienced a renewed sense of our caring for each other. We popped a cork from a bottle of champagne and raised our glasses to one another: "To life!"

. . . .

PLAY IT AGAIN, SAM

Once you get beyond the natural fear of death, you can all start to have some fun with the planning. At our first family conference, I led off by saying, "I don't want organ music. I hate organ music!"

And Dad said, "Me too, and I want a saxophone at my funeral."

"A saxophone?" my mother and I shouted.

"That's right. You know, I played the clarinet when I was young, but I've always loved the saxophone. I want it playing that song they played on the ship when we sailed to Alaska. What was it? Ah yes, 'Up the Lazy River.'"

Well, you can bet that when the time comes we're going to make sure a saxophonist is playing for Dad. Of course, it would never have occurred to us on our own. If we hadn't gotten together to discuss these "morbid" plans, we'd never have thought of this delightful way to celebrate my father's life.

— Sheila

. . . .

Ideally, you will want to hold such a conference while everyone in the family is in good health. But if someone is elderly or terminally ill, try to be brave enough to suggest the idea anyway. If you present it as a group project, you'll take the focus away from the oncoming death. Here are some suggestions:

❏ **Appoint someone as the recording secretary**
You don't want to be racking your brains years from now, trying to remember what Grandpa said about caskets. Have a keen-eared participant take notes for everyone.

❏ **Begin with a general discussion**
Within the family — even between spouses — there may be strong differences of opinion on issues like viewing or cremation. Your objective is not to bring everyone around to the same opinions, but you certainly do want to know whether the others would honor your requests if their own prefer-

ences are different. For instance, if you want to be buried and your husband prefers cremation, what would each of you do if the other died first?

❏ **Listen to individual requests**

One by one, go around the table and ask each person to state his or her wishes on every issue that is important to them. If you like, include special requests for the service — anything at all — even who not to invite to give the eulogy. Your volunteer secretary can take notes and type them up later for distribution.

❏ **Sign or witness any important papers**

This is the perfect opportunity to sign and witness wills, organ donor cards, and bequeathal certificates.

Organizing the Paperwork

Organizing the paperwork of your life — the legal documents, certificates, tax records, and all — can be daunting to those of us who use the "shoe box" method of accounting. Once established, however, a home filing system is relatively easy to maintain. Mastering the paper tiger has a double benefit: well-ordered records are a blessing to your survivors, and they make life much easier for you. Here's how to set up a home filing system:

1. Purchase a small filing cabinet and file folders, or a simple, expandable cardboard filer. Use this filing cabinet or filer to store all legal documents and other important papers that are not stored in a safety deposit box or other location outside your home.

2. Buy a looseleaf binder and some tab dividers. You'll use this binder to record information for your survivors under various categories. On three of the dividers, write "Death and Estate Information," "Financial and Legal Information," and "Personal Information."

3. Now, using the lists below, take a fresh sheet of paper for every category that you want to include in the binder. Write the name of the category (for example, "Stocks and Bonds") at the top of the sheet and use the sheet to describe anything at all you want to tell your survivors about this item. Also give the location of any important papers relevant to this category. Some papers may be stored in your home filing system, others at the lawyer's office, safety deposit box, and so on.

4. Tell your spouse, lawyer, executor, or someone close to you about the binder and where you keep it.

5. Get into the habit of updating the binder regularly — when you do your taxes, for instance, or whenever you review your will. Needless to say, store the binder in a safe place.

If you record this information on a computer it is, of course, even easier to update. Be sure to date and print out the revisions and put them in your binder. Once again, make this system your own. Combine categories, ignore the ones that don't work for you, create new ones. The objective is not to become a slave to some impossible system, but rather to simplify your dealings with the essential paperwork of life. Here are some suggested categories:

Death and estate information

❏ **Bequeathal certificate**
Say where the bequeathal certificate is stored and give the name and phone number of the medical institution with which it is filed.

❏ **Funeral arrangements**
Include a list of your wishes, and any information about items such as a prepaid funeral or cemetery plot.

❏ **Organ donor card**
Either include a copy of the organ donor card you carry in your wallet, or make mention of it here. Also give the name and phone number of the institution to be called.

❏ **Living Will**
Note the location of the Living Will you have signed. Mention whether or not you have spoken to your doctor about your wishes.

❏ **Will**
Note the date of your latest will and its location; the executor's name, address, and phone number; and the lawyer's name, address, and phone number.

Financial and legal information

❏ **Accountant**
Note your accountant's name, address, and phone number, and describe what services he or she usually performs for you. For example, tax returns only, or full business and personal accounting.

❏ **Banking information**
List the name, address, and phone number of each bank, trust company, or credit union in which you have funds deposited. List the account numbers and type of account for each. Note the location of bank books, check books, and bank statements. Include information on term deposits.

❑ **Bills**

Note where your current and paid bills are kept. If you have written post-dated checks, list the payee and amounts. Also mention any ongoing contractual obligations, such as a gardening service or cable TV.

❑ **Business ownership or partnership agreements**

If you have any such agreements, mention the key facts here (for example, partners' names and phone numbers) and give the location of the documents.

❑ **Citizenship papers**

Note your country of origin, the date of your change of citizenship, and the location of the papers.

❑ **Charitable foundations, gifts, or trusts**

If you have any ongoing commitments — of time or money — to charitable or other organizations, describe them here, with relevant names, addresses, and phone numbers.

❑ **Credit cards**

List the location of each credit card, the name of the credit card issuer, and the account number.

❑ **Insurance policies**

List your insurance policies in every category: life, disability, group, house, tenant's, auto, and fire. For each policy, note the name of the insurance company, the policy number, the primary and contingent beneficiary, the original amount of the policy, and the name, address, and phone number of the insurance agent.

❑ **Lawyer**

Note your lawyer's name, address, and phone number. Briefly describe any important current activity on your behalf, such as a suit against a former employer for wrongful dismissal, or a divorce action.

❑ **Lease or rental information**

Note the location of your lease or rental agreement. Give the name, address, and phone number of your landlord, the amount and date of the security deposit, the amount of the monthly rent and when it is due.

❑ **Loans payable**

Give the location of any loan papers or promissory notes and mention the payment due dates and amounts.

❑ **Memberships and subscriptions**

List any social groups, clubs, sports organizations, or religious groups you belong to. Note any magazine subscriptions or book or music club memberships.

❑ **Military discharge papers**

Note rank, serial number, branch of the services, dates joined and discharged, and give the location of the papers.

❑ **Mortgages**

Give the location of any mortgages and mention the payment due dates and amounts.

❑ **Pensions**

Provide information on pensions, including government, work, and private plans.

❑ **Real estate**

Give the address and legal description of all property owned, the date of acquisition, cost, and information on the mortgage holder, the original amount of the mortgage, and whether you have mortgage insurance.

❑ **Retirement income**

Include information on all sources of retirement income, including Independent Retirement Accounts and the Keogh Plan (United States), and Registered Retirement Savings Plans (Canada). For each plan, list the type of plan, insurer, policy number, primary and contingent beneficiary, maturity date, and amount payable.

❑ **Safety deposit box**

Note the name of the institution and address where the box is located. Give the name, address, and phone number of everyone with access to the box, and the location of all keys.

❑ **Social security or social insurance numbers**

List the social security (U.S.) or social insurance (Canada) numbers for everyone in the family. These numbers are needed to collect benefits after death.

❑ **Stocks and bonds**

Give the name, address, and phone number of your broker, and your account number. For each stock or bond, give the number owned, the name and address of the issuing company or government, the certificate numbers, the type of stock or bond, date acquired, acquisition cost, the location of the certificates, and the maturity or expiration dates.

❑ **Tax records**

Give the location of your old tax returns plus receipts and information for the current year.

❑ **Union benefits**

Give the name, address, and phone number of the union business agent, and details of any benefits your beneficiary will receive upon your death.

❏ **Vehicle title and registration**
Give the location of the title or bill of sale and registration papers for all cars, trailers, motorcycles, trucks, boats, and other vehicles.

Personal information

❏ **Birth and marriage certificates**
Include information on your, spouse's, and your children's birth certificates, as well as the birth date and place of your parents, and your mother's maiden name (needed for your own death certificate). If you are divorced, give the location of the divorce papers. They may be needed to settle your estate.

❏ **Children's information**
If both you and your spouse were killed together in an accident, the children's guardian would need a tremendous amount of information to keep their lives in order. Include the name, address, and phone number of the school, and of all the important people in their lives: teachers, close friends, doctors, dentist, organization, and more. Now stop to think about anything else you would want the guardian to know: Joey's fear of snakes, for instance, or the promise you made to Alison of her own car when she turns 18.

❏ **Guarantees and warranties**
Tell your survivors where you keep the guarantees and instruction booklets for all your appliances and equipment — stereo, microwave, VCR, computer, and the rest.

❏ **Medical information**
Give the name, address, and phone number for all your doctors including the eye doctor, and dentist. Give any information that would be useful in a crisis, for instance, allergies to drugs, or your MedicAlert condition.

❏ **Names and numbers**
On this sheet, list the names and numbers of people you would want to be notified of your death, or give the usual location of your address book.

❏ **Passport**
Give the location of the passports of everyone in the family.

❏ **Religious or spiritual affiliation**
Give the name, address, and phone number of your church or spiritual group and the name of the clergyperson or leader.

❑ **Valuables**

If you have not included a list of valuables in your will, do so here: jewelry, furs, collections, antiques. Include the location of each valuable, and its acquisition date and cost.

Alberta's Expected Home Death Program

Since 1980 in the province of Alberta, residents have been able — with the help of their doctor — to preregister their own impending death or the death of a terminally ill loved one. The little-known program allows the patient to die with dignity, without the intervention of ambulance crews, police, or doctors. The only legal requirement is that a doctor must be called within 48 hours to sign a death certificate.

. . . .

GET CLOSE TO EACH OTHER RIGHT NOW

"We had such a close relationship with my dad, that we never had any regrets after he died. We have such great memories of him and the good times we had together. Obviously, I'd rather he was still living, but at least I never had to think, 'If only I'd been a better son.'

We all got along so well. We were really close as a family — doing things together, talking very openly, and treating each other as equals. If I could offer any advice to other people it would be: Don't procrastinate. Get close to each other right now, today, and show respect for each other. You'll still grieve, but you won't have any regrets."

— Mark Montizambert, *Vancouver, British Columbia*

. . . .

SHE THREW HER OWN GOODBYE PARTY

At 4:30 a.m. January 7, 1994 Sue Beischer woke up and noticed something important. She wasn't in pain.

The 40-year-old Vancouver Island woman had been suffering greatly from incurable ovarian cancer. But her doctor had prescribed a 72-hour "pain patch" that delivers an analgesic pain killer. Sue felt strong and well-rested. She decided to throw herself a party.

She booked a hotel and music, arranged for food, and asked for help in organizing the invitations and flowers. With only one week's notice, more than 800 people showed up. They came from as far away as Hawaii. They danced until one in the morning.

Through the party, Sue gave her friends and family the opportunity to celebrate their friendship with her while she was still there to celebrate with them.

As her friend Cairine Green said: "Sue redefined our concept of the ritual of dying. She took the concept of grief and put it at some other level. . . She took every piece of her life and put it together in one night."

- From a story by Star Weiss, *The Vancouver Sun, January 28, 1994*

. . . .

Chapter 14 🌿

Remembering

In this final chapter, we'll look at grief, love, and remembrance. The topics are

- ▸ Healing your grief
- ▸ Traditional ways to remember
- ▸ Gifts and foundations
- ▸ Writing about your memories
- ▸ Creating a memory book
- ▸ Creating a memory video
- ▸ Memorials on the Internet
- ▸ Naming a star

There are many options given here. Use only the ones that appeal to you, or simply take one as a starting point to spark fresh ideas of your own.

DEEP GRIEF

"If you love deeply, you will grieve deeply. If you deny your grief, you deny the reality of the love you felt."

—Diana McKendree

Healing Your Grief

This section is about healing your grief. The memories, experiences, and feelings you shared together belong — now — to no one else but you. Your way of grieving, too, will be uniquely yours.

You may relentlessly seek out people to talk to, to re-tell the story of the dying and the death, or you may present a stoic face to the world and only express your grief in private moments. You may cry every day for months — or not cry at all until suddenly, months from now, something trivial triggers a flood of tears and you know you are crying for this loss.

How do you climb back out of the sea of grief and despair? How do you stop the pain? The answer is: do not try. Do not seek to escape the pain. Only by embracing your grief, holding it gently, will you know release.

Feel the grief. Feel the rage, and the fear, and the overwhelming sense of loss that this death brings to you. Weep as often as you need to. Pound a pillow until there's nothing left to pound. Drive to an isolated spot, roll up your car windows, and scream out your frustration and fear. Let your defenses drift away. Stop fighting the pain. Even, see the pain as your friend. See your acceptance of the pain as the safest way to inner peace, acceptance of the death, and love of the life you are living today.

Returning to life

Later, when some time has passed, reach out to life again. Sometimes we stay too long in the pain, fearing that to let it go will mean we no longer miss or love the one who has died. But think of what you loved about that person. Was it not her aliveness, her joy, or his unique way of reaching out to the world around him? And did he or she not love you for the same reasons? Expressing your own aliveness today is a way to show your love — for everyone you love now, and have ever loved.

Remember, too, that you will never go "back to normal," back to the way things were. You can only go forward into your new life. As you travel the often bumpy road from grief to healing, you will sometimes run from the pain, sometimes pretend it isn't there, sometimes embrace it, and eventually walk beyond the pain into a richer, more compassionate life than you have ever known.

· ·

ACKNOWLEDGING THE DEATH AND LOSS

"Another practice that many have found useful is to put a photograph of the departed loved one on a table, perhaps with a candle and some incense next to it, so that each day for the first week or two after death one may sit for half an hour or so with the loved one and speak to him of the love that has been shared and the need for him to continue on his journey. After ten days or so (as the heart dictates), the practice may be carried out only on a weekly basis, on the anniversary of the death, for a total of seven weeks. This is a skillful means both for the departed and for the individual who may be in grief, for it allows a letting go and a sending on that is skillful for both. It allows the finishing of business while a recognition of death and loss is fully acknowledged."
— Stephen Levine, *Who Dies?*

· ·

In practical terms, what can you do, right now, to heal your grief? Here are a few suggestions.

❑ **Read about death, dying, and grieving**
   There are many excellent books on bereavement and coping with grief — everything from sociological studies by academics to compelling first-person accounts by people just like you who have suffered a loss.

There are books especially for the survivors of someone who has chosen suicide, for parents who've lost a baby at birth or through miscarriage, books for widows and widowers, books for those who've lost someone to cancer, and more.

Experienced librarians can help you choose exactly the right book. As well, most bookstores have a selection of the most popular and recent titles. Several fine audiotapes are now available as well.

❏ **Find a support group**

In most communities there are support groups for those who are grieving. These groups may be run by a church or a nonprofit society, or they may be simply a group of people in a similar situation who have banded together on their own.

You may want to seek out a group that deals specifically with your situation: for instance, Compassionate Friends, for parents of children who have died, or Widows Helping Widows, or a group for the survivors of someone who has committed suicide.

❏ **Start a support group**

If you can't find a support group that meets your needs, consider starting one yourself. Place a small ad in the "Personals" section of your newspaper inviting others to call you. For example: "Have you lost a family member to suicide? New support group starting. Will meet Thursdays at 7:30. Call Anna at 555-1234." Doug Manning's book, *Comforting Those Who Grieve,* is a good source of ideas on how to start a support group and what to talk about at meetings.

❏ **Talk to friends**

A friend who can quietly listen is worth her weight in gold. You may find that not everyone has the confidence and skill to support you in your grief. Some friends may be uncomfortable with your pain and want you to "get over it" quickly. Others may make insensitive remarks or even drift away from you, just when you need them most. Even though you may feel hurt or confused by such behavior, try to understand that they are only showing their own fear and pain. You can even use these occasions to learn forgiveness and compassion.

The bonus, of course, is that the more understanding you show to others, the more understanding you will draw into your own life.

❏ **Talk to professional counselors**

Sometimes we need more help than our friends can give us. If the pain seems unbearable — even to be getting worse — do seek professional help. A trained therapist can help you shed light on the beliefs and fears that are causing so much pain. You can learn to take all that energy, which is going into hurting, and transform it into joyful, loving energy.

Many therapists specialize in grief counseling. If you're not comfortable with the first therapist you find, seek out another whose style and values are closer to your own. You deserve the best of care.

❑ **Listen to sad songs**

In Denver, Colorado, psychologist Larry Huston offers a workshop called "Country Mourning" to help people work through grief. "Country music holds the seeds of healing," says Huston. "To heal hurt, you have to move toward pain, not away from it." He recommends tunes like Patsy Cline's *Crazy* or Hank Williams' *She's Long Gone Lonesome Blues.* Listening to these mournful songs, says Huston, "the listener is reassured that he or she is not alone in this world."

❑ **Be good to yourself**

Find active ways to love yourself. Go for long walks, buy yourself a bouquet of roses, get tickets for the hot new play in town, have friends in for a barbecue, sign up for a night school massage course, take up oil painting. Do something you've always wanted to do. Do whatever makes you feel good about you.

For children suffering the loss of a parent, bedtime can be especially hard. One young mother decided to buy a good tape recorder and a selection of children's tapes and soothing music. Each night, she let her two children take turns choosing a favorite tape to listen to in the half hour before bedtime. All three were comforted by this new ritual.

❑ **Reach out to others**

Time and again, survivors have said that what really helped them the most was when they reached out to others. Could you volunteer to teach adult illiterates to read? Help an elderly friend put in a garden? Bring baking to a shut-in? Maybe the experience you've gained through this death would make you a valuable resource to someone going through the same thing. You have a tremendous amount to give, and there are many who would welcome your help.

Traditional Ways to Remember

The rituals and ceremonies of remembrance can be healing too. Here are some possibilities for you:

❑ **Visit the cemetery or mausoleum**

For some people, visiting the cemetery is a way to express their grief and love. You might plant a bush or bulbs at the gravesite. Then, caring for the plants becomes an opportunity to grieve by taking action. If it feels like a duty or is too painful to visit the grave, don't go. It is just as meaningful to grieve at home, where your memories of the person are stronger.

❏ **Mark the first anniversary of the death**

The first anniversary can be a difficult time. You might want to mark it in a special way. This doesn't have to be a sad or formal ceremony. Perhaps Dad's favorite meal was steak and scalloped potatoes, so you prepare a big feed of them for family and friends. After dinner, you spend a little time together remembering Dad and reliving the days of his life.

Or perhaps the child you have lost loved to ice-skate. On the anniversary of the death, you could bundle up the whole family and spend the afternoon at the skating rink.

❏ **Remember the birthday**

My grandmother died at age 93. Seven years later we had a small ceremony to mark the day she would have celebrated her 100th birthday.

❏ **Have prayers or Masses said**

You may arrange for prayers or a Mass on the anniversary of the death, a birthday, or "just because" you want to. It can be a source of strength to know that the community of believers to which you belong are joining together in prayers for your loved one.

❏ **Place a memorial ad in the newspaper**

Most newspapers include a memorial column after the obituaries. The classified ad staff will usually help you write it, or they may have a booklet of suitable poems.

Gifts and Foundations

A gift to a charitable group or favorite cause is a special and lasting way to celebrate the life of someone you loved. There are so many worthy recipients in so many fields: health care, education, social services, spirituality, community improvement, the arts, the environment, and research.

There are three types of gift-giving: a direct, one-time gift to a charitable group or cause, a contribution to an ongoing fund within a community foundation, and the establishment of a private foundation.

A gift does not have to be large. The money you would have spent for a birthday or anniversary gift for your special person can be used to make your donation.

A direct gift usually benefits the recipient on one occasion; a private foundation continues the donor's generosity for many years. For instance, as a memorial to a doctor, you could establish a scholarship foundation to assist students who intend to become general practitioners. To honor a woman who spent her last months in a hospice, you might establish a fund to aid in research for care of the dying.

Private foundations

The private foundation offers an organized approach to gift-giving. It may exist for only one purpose or for a limited time, or it may carry on in perpetuity, changing its goals to meet the changing needs of society. The private foundation is the ideal way for dedicated philanthropists to focus their charitable pursuits efficiently. It allows you to zero in on a clearly defined area of interest.

Both gifts and foundations are recognized as an indispensable supplement to government funding. As such, they receive preferential tax treatment.

To set up the foundation, you must

1. Establish the legal form the foundation is to take

2. Register the foundation as a charity under the guidelines set by the tax department.

An excellent booklet published by The Canadian Centre for Philanthropy (Goodman and Carr, *Establishing a Private Foundation*) strips away the complexities of establishing and administering a private foundation. Although the tax and legal information applies specifically to Canadians, the overall discussion will be useful to Americans as well. As Goodman and Carr point out, there is no legal minimum amount of money for the establishment of a foundation. In Canada, approximately 75 percent of all foundations hold assets with a value of less than $500,000, and over half of all foundations give less than $25,000 annually.

You can also set up a foundation with a small sum, with the intention of adding to it periodically with contributions from living family members or from bequests.

. . . .

YOU LIVE FOREVER

"Know this: when you care, when you fight injustices and when you love, you live forever."
—Phil Wilson

. . . .

Community foundations

If you want to avoid the expense and administrative responsibility of setting up a private foundation, making a contribution to an established community foundation could be your answer. (Call your library for a list of foundations.)

The community foundation is an amalgamation of many gifts from individuals, families, businesses, other charitable foundations, and estates. The overall goal of the community foundation is to enhance the quality of life within its own neighborhood.

You can contribute either to the general holdings of the fund, or name a special new fund within the foundation. This named fund would be recognized in the annual reports and other publicity of the community foundation.

In the same way, some charitable organizations allow you to contribute either to the general fund or to create a new endowment fund as a living memorial.

. . . .

THE VALUE OF PRIVATE PHILANTHROPY

"Private philanthropy continues to be one of the most powerful forces for improving the social order in our society. Universities, religious orders, research laboratories, hospitals, museums, orchestras, and many other organizations are sustained by charitable giving. There can be no doubt that most of the progress achieved in a wide variety of areas of our increasingly complex community could never have happened without private resources, from some of the most exciting and far-reaching medical advances to providing life-sustaining funds to our poorest and neediest."
— Wolfe Goodman and Howard Carr, *Establishing a Private Foundation*

. . . .

Writing About Your Memories

Many people — even those who haven't written since high school English class — have turned to writing both as an outlet for grief, and a way to celebrate the life of the one who is gone. Here are some suggestions for those who want to use this powerful tool.

❏ **Keep a diary or journal**
Even if you don't consider yourself a writer, think about keeping a journal for the next few months. A private journal is the ideal place to write out your grief, anger, and self-pity — and your cherished memories.

The journal itself doesn't have to be fancy. If the book you are trying to write in is beautifully bound with gold-trimmed pages, you may be too intimidated to write much. A child's exercise book may be just right, or a stenographer's pad, or a loose-leaf binder. A computer gives you the freedom to change and edit whatever you've written. Whatever tool you use, give yourself permission to write absolutely anything — including your most hateful and angry thoughts — knowing that you can throw them away later, while keeping the record of your good memories.

❏ **Write a memorial poem or story or song**
A poem, story, or song is a uniquely personal way to remember. What you write could be just for yourself, or you may want to share it with others. Ann Eck's family in Montana put together a booklet for friends and family several months after Ann's death. The booklet included a smiling photograph on the cover, prayers from the service, and excerpts from the many letters Ann's husband, Laurence, had received.

As Laurence says: "Preparing the booklet helped all of us, as therapy for our grief, to move ahead in a positive fashion, while giving us an opportunity to express our feelings and record them."

. . . .

"SWEET CHARLIE"

"When my father died last year after spending his last years in the Gorge Hospital, we wanted to do something that would be appreciated by the staff members who cared for dad, as well as present and future residents. We asked staff for their suggestions and they agreed on a portable radio/CD player. We purchased a good quality machine and added a couple of CDs and placed a small plaque on the player, dedicating it in dad's name. This has proven to be a popular gift.

An equally appreciated effort started out to be a picture board that I put together for dad. It was entitled 'Charlie Clarke — this is your life' and contained pictures of dad and his family throughout his life. The idea was to make dad proud of his life and his family, but it turned out to serve another useful purpose. It told the staff who Charlie Clarke was and they came to know their "Sweet Charlie" as a person with an interesting and happy life rather than simply an old man waiting to die.

When dad died and I was cleaning out his belongings, a nurse asked if I would leave the picture board as an example for other families to emulate. It now occupies wall space and one staff member recently told us that it not only helps them to suggest similar ideas to families but also helps the families to overcome the guilt of placing loved ones in a nursing home.

It was heartwarming to hear that such a simple idea has become a worthwhile suggestion.

—Bob Clarke, *Victoria, British Columbia*

. . . .

❏ **Write a letter to the one you've lost**

Especially if there are things you wish you'd said or done before the death, writing a letter to the person can help. Pour out your heart. Say everything you always wanted to say — things you didn't even know you felt. Once you've done that, you might write what you imagine his or her reply to you would be.

❏ **Make lists**

List all the things you want to remember about the person. List everything you wish you'd said or done (or wish you hadn't). Then, make a list of everything you are glad you said or did. Make a list of every way in which your life will be disrupted by this death. (For example: "Now there's no one who remembers the excitement of Connie's first tooth" or "I'll have to learn to drive now" or "Who will tell me when I need a haircut?") Make a list of everything that was wrong with the service (and then list everything that was right).

❏ **Write — or even speak out loud — a dialogue with the person**

Making up a dialogue with the person may cause you to feel extraordinarily close to the other again. The process often yields startling insights as well. Play with the dialogue. Don't have any expectations about where it will lead you. For example, here's a young wife talking with her late husband:

Me: *How could you do this to me, John? Leaving me alone with 2 kids, and not enough insurance, and you're only 38. I told you to see the doctor about your chest pains. I can't believe this has happened to me. I hurt so much.*

John: *Sorry sweetheart, I really am. I should have listened to you. But gee, you wouldn't believe the great golfing up here.*

Me: *Don't joke with me, damn it! It makes me miss you even more . . . .*

Creating a Memory Book

Creating a Memory Book is another special way to remember the dead. A Memory Book can contain anything that reminds you of the person: writing, photographs, remembrances from other people, special condolence letters, writings or objects created by or for the person, artwork, awards, certificates, medals, and postcards.

If you have children who are not old enough to write, let them tell you their memories while you tape record or write them down. Or perhaps the child could do a special drawing of what the person meant to her.

A wonderful way for workplace colleagues to focus their grief is to create a book of memories for the family. Many people are not aware of their loved one's accomplishments and impact at their workplace. It's a way for you and your co-workers to express your grief, while at the same time creating a precious memento for the family.

. . . .

A PICTURE ALBUM TO HONOR MOM'S LIFE

"A picture album we put together to honor Mom's life had this notation under a picture of the empty wheelchair: '— the cane, the walker, and finally, the damned wheelchair were an affront to Mom's feeling of independence — it was as though Mom decided — enough is enough! She was tired of the pain and forced inactivity — so — she gathered her family around her very subtly, wrote her letters, and made her phone calls and then — on Jan. 3, 1988, in her own bed, in her own house, Mom passed on into the great unknown — as inquisitive about this ultimate adventure as she was about everything in this life!"

— Bob Clarke, *Victoria, British Columbia*

. . . .

What kind of book to use

If you plan to tape or glue objects into the Memory Book, a big scrapbook — the kind children use in art class — is ideal. A photograph album is another possibility. If you just want to write, a bound book with blank pages might be best. You can find blank books in many book and stationery stores.

What to write or include

In the Memory Book, tell the story of your relationship: how you met, what you liked about each other, the important moments you shared, what you liked to do together, what you fought about, what you learned from the person.

Talk about how it felt to be together, expressions he characteristically used, how she would always touch your cheek to say goodbye, the taste of his barbecued hamburgers, the time you cried together over a lost promotion.

What about newspaper clippings? For example: the time he won a swimming competition, the announcement of your engagement, or a letter to the editor that was published.

Is there a family tree you could add to the book? You might want to include old letters and photographs, organized either chronologically or according to themes. For example: "Marlene at Home," "On the Job," "Our Vacations."

Are there any family traditions or legends you want to describe? Perhaps a favorite cookie recipe, his political views, her athletic skills, a few words about what you learned from him. The Memory Book can reflect your picture of the person, or that person's place in the world. It is entirely your own creation.

If you plan to do a Memory Book, do it soon. You want to capture the essence of the person now, while your memories are still fresh. Then you will no longer have to be afraid you will forget the person you loved so much.

. . . .

REMEMBERING PEACEFULLY

"It is not a question of forgetting, but of regaining the capacity to remember peacefully."
— Michael Simpson, *The Facts of Death*

. . . .

Creating a Memory Video

A home video is an audiovisual version of the Memory Book. If you have children or grandchildren, this is an ideal way to involve them in remembering. They will probably want to take over the project — directing, producing, and filming the video.

There's no need to buy a video camera. If you can't borrow one, many video stores will rent you one for a day. You can even rent a VCR unit on which to play back the video. You may also want to rent a separate microphone, an extra battery, and a battery charger. The only thing you need to buy is a blank video tape.

Planning the video

You certainly don't need a complete script for your Memory Video, with every word written down and rehearsed. But you do need some idea of who will be speaking, what you'll be filming, and in what order.

Keep in mind that whatever you record, stays recorded, and in exactly that order — unless you have the equipment and skills to edit the tape. (This means you won't want to record the kids fooling around as they learn to operate the camera, nor will you want 10 minutes of someone's tears.)

Have a least an outline for a script. Is the video just for you? Or will it be for your children, all your friends, and family? How do you want your audience to feel after viewing the video? Can you find some interesting locations and other people to participate? How about a few scenes in Dad's workroom, or Sarah's nursery, with Joey's soccer buddies, or Mom's bridge club?

Will you or someone else narrate the video? A narrator could introduce the video, tell some basic facts, and link each segment to the next. You may want to include special props, such as a graduation diploma or bronzed baby shoes.

Finding a theme

See if you can come up with a "theme" — a basic framework to tie all your facts together. The theme might be summed up in a title you give to the video. For example, "The Many Sides of Daisy Peterson" (the video shows her as wife, mother, sister, volunteer, jogger . . .). Or: "Gerry Bukowski, Mountain-Climber" (about a man who tackled mountains, both in his beloved hobby of rock-climbing and in his battle with cancer).

Again, who is the video for? If it is only for you, it can be as personal and private and full of grief as you like. If you want to show it to other people, plan the script with your audience in mind.

Try to give the video a structure, just like a story. See if you can come up with an attention-getting beginning, a satisfying ending, and continuity with your theme throughout the video. For example, suppose your theme (and your title) is "Amanda Davies: The Lady with the Big Heart." You might start quietly by showing a montage of photos of Amanda, as you tell a story that clearly illustrates her good-heartedness. You could then carry on the theme with interviews of family and friends, and close with a group shot outside on the lawn, showing all Amanda's family, joined in their love for her.

Adding sound

You could have music playing in the background: a teenager's favorite rock group, perhaps, or simply someone whistling. The music could be coming from an audiotape, or CD player, or someone playing the piano or guitar.

You might want to record background sounds for some of your images: the laughter of children playing at a favorite beach, for instance, or even the opening music from a favorite TV show.

While you're at it, why not create a video of your living family and friends? Our family cherishes the audio tape we made during the celebration of Grandma's 90th birthday, another of Grandma telling her favorite stories, the family-history video my sister and I made in honor of our parents' 40th wedding anniversary, and the "This is Your Life" video my husband Bob and I made for Dad's 80th birthday.

A Memory Video can be a wonderful legacy for your family for generations to come.

Memorials on the Internet

Since early 1994, mourners have been able to express their grief by memorializing their loved ones on the Internet. (Locations are given here with the reminder that sites disappear and addresses change frequently on the Internet.) One of the most popular sites is the Virtual Memorial Garden, which is at (http://catless.ncl.ac.uk/VMG). Lindsay Marshall, a computer science lecturer in Newcastle in the United Kingdom, designed the site as "a place where people can celebrate their family, friends, and pets and tell the rest of us about them and why there were special." At this writing, the Virtual Memorial Garden has room for only a brief amount of text for each submission and no graphics.

In the Worldwide Cemetery (http://www.cemetery.org), Net users can present whole memorial pages, including images and sound for a one-time fee. The Garden of Remembrance (http://www.islandnet.com/ ~ deathnet/gate.html) charges a yearly maintenance fee. Users can upload photos, music and voice recordings and video clips to memorialize loved ones.

Naming a Star

When police officer Larry Young was killed senselessly in a drug bust gone wrong, his fellow officers "purchased" a star in his name as a gift to his widow and two children. The family received a certificate from the International Star Registry (a private business) that the star which bears the star map designation Hercules RA 16h 56m 32sd 38 long. 15 lat. is now called Larry T. Young. The gift means a great deal to the family and friends who loved him.

REMEMBERING EDDIE

This remembrance of a beloved friend was written more than 15 years after his death.

"For years I'd known that I would probably outlive my friend, but even so I wasn't prepared for the call when it came. Three weeks earlier, my son and I had hitchhiked across Vancouver Island to the little fishing village where Hope and Eddie went to live after he lost his sight and dropped out of graduate school. Eddie tried having people read the philosophy books to him for a few months after the vision was gone, and there was no shortage of pretty young undergraduates who were willing. This was the early seventies, and a bearded dude who looked like a Hell's Angel, claimed to have IRA connections, and had a steel-trap mind as well, had lots of ladies hanging around for the action.

No, I wasn't one of them. For one thing, I had met Hope and Eddie a decade earlier in a little town half a continent away, where Eddie wore a tie to work every day, and Hope and I were called 'Mrs.' by rooms full of little kids. I loved him dearly and I also knew everything about him, and he knew everything about me. Anyway, in the end he gave away most of his books, hundreds of them, and moved to Ucluelet on the west coast of Vancouver Island.

On that last visit, I woke up in the middle of the night. Through the wall, Eddie was groaning. When I tiptoed in, I saw Hope sound asleep on a little cot at the end of their double bed, not waking up at all even though she was so close to him. He was groaning because he'd rolled over on his own arm, and with only one foot left and that on the side paralyzed by the stroke, he couldn't move back without help. I lifted him over, heavy as he was, and he fell back to sleep right away. I lay awake for a while, thinking about how it could feel to be inside that body, and about how Hope could be so exhausted that she wouldn't even hear him.

The morning of the funeral, Carla and I went over to the Island on the ferry. She was one of Eddie's pretty ladies. She was also gentle and smart. We were sitting out on the deck during the crossing, and a beer bottle came flying out of the cabin behind us and over our heads. It was the kind of thing that Eddie would have liked. He would have gone inside and joined the party.

The special thing about Eddie was that he could see good in people in many forms. Some good people loved partying, some were intellectuals, some were shy and some were flamboyant. Eddie would see what was special and good about each one, and create a mythology to explain and enhance that friend to the others.

When Carla and I arrived at the little bungalow where Eddie and Hope had lived, the living room was full of people from Vancouver. Robert, who had been a draughtsman back East, and was now a fisherman, had flown to Tofino, and then rented a Cadillac to drive down the Island. Eddie would have loved that. He always approved of the grand gesture. Hope wasn't there, but one of Eddie's pretty ladies from Toronto was, her face swollen from crying. She had come out to the Island the week before, and she had been the one who found him dead.

Hope was with Eddie's mother, at the undertaker's. They were looking at him for the last time. Then the casket would be closed and brought from Alberni to the Lutheran church.

Some of Eddie's friends were not comfortable about going to the church. This was clearly Eddie's mother's idea, and Eddie's mother had never approved of much about the last ten years of Eddie's life — the drugs, the ladies, the drinking in spite of the diabetes and the stroke and the amputated foot. Someone said that Eddie's mom had even arranged for the local Lutheran pastor to give communion at the house on her last visit. Did Eddie take it? No one knew.

About a quarter to three, Robert and some of the others took out their instruments. We sang 'May the Circle be Unbroken,' and then we crowded into the cars and went to the church.

Robert and Jerome and Stu and Joe Stranger took their places up near the minister. Carla and I sat farther back. We weren't prepared for the crowd at that church. The pews were filled with people from the village, sober and solid-looking. Hope and Eddie's mother were at the front. When Hope turned around, her face was another surprise. She was glowing and peaceful. She had given most of her life so far to making him happy. I couldn't imagine her in a world without him."

— Percilla Groves, *Vancouver, British Columbia*

· ·

Resources

This section includes a selection of resources for survivors. The categories are

▸ Books

▸ Burial boxes

▸ Legal expense plans

▸ Support groups

Books

The books listed below are meant to help you renew and re-create all the aspects of your life after this death — everything from your finances to your emotions to your work life.

Death, dying, and grief

There are many fine books on grief — written for every age, and every situation. Your librarian or bookseller can help you select the books for your unique needs. If you can't find what you're looking for, Rainbow Connection has over 400 books, videos and audiotapes about dying, death, and grief. Write to Rainbow Connection, 477 Hannah Branch Road, Burnsville, NC 28714 and ask for the two free catalogs (for Rainbow Connection and Compassion Books). Phone (828) 675-9670 or fax (828) 675-9687. Here are just a few to watch for:

▸ Caine, Lynn. *Widow* and *Being a Widow* (stories and advice for the newly widowed).

▸ Deits, Bob. *Life After Loss* (a reassuring, readable guide for adults)

▸ Dykstra, Robert. *She Never Said Good-bye: One Man's Journey Through Loss* (a man's struggle to understand his wife's suicide).

▸ Elmer, Lon. *Why Her? Why Now? A Man's Journey Through Love and Grief.*

- Feinberg, Linda. *I'm Grieving As Fast As I Can* (especially for younger widowed people).

- Fitzgerald, Helen. *The Mourning Handbook* (Fitzgerald draws from much experience to offer comprehensive, compassionate advice).

- Grollman, Earl A. *What Helped Me When My Loved One Died* (moving personal stories from people of all ages who have lost a loved one).

- Menten, Ted. *After Goodbye* (a collection of stories about love and loss).

- Morgan, Ernest. *Dealing Creatively with Death* (This classic work by a North Carolina Quaker includes not just information on bereavement, but chapters on everything from the right-to-die movement to death ceremonies. Morgan has a sensible, openhearted approach to death that we all can learn from.)

- Sanders, Catherine. *How to Survive the Loss of a Child* (written by a psychologist who has herself lost a child).

- Tatelbaum, Judy. *The Courage to Grieve* (how to feel your grief and come out the other side).

- Viorst, Judith. *The Tenth Good Thing About Barney* (classic and moving picture story about the loss of a beloved pet helps young children understand grief and death)

Financial health

- Chilton, David. *The Wealthy Barber.* Prima, 1995.

  One of the most popular books on personal money management ever written. Using the engaging story of Roy, the wealthy barber, dispensing down-home advice to his customers, Chilton offers easy-to-implement strategies that ordinary people can use to comfortably build their own wealth.

- Mundis, Jerrold. *How to Get Out of Debt, Stay Out of Debt & Live Prosperously.* Bantam, 1990.

  You don't have to be a debtor to profit from this delightfully upbeat book. As Mundis says: "This isn't about eating cat food and working harder." Using easy, practical tools such as Action Lists and Spending Plans (which are much friendlier than budgets), the book is a step-by-step guide to taking charge of your financial life.

Foundations

▸ Goodman, Wolfe, and Howard Carr. *Establishing a Private Foundation.* The Canadian Centre for Philanthropy, 1987.

A short, practical guide to setting up and administering a private charitable foundation. Phone: (416) 597-2293. Web: *www.ccp.ca*

Legal questions

▸ Dacey, Norman F. *How to Avoid Probate — 5th edition.* New York: HarperPerennial, 1993. (Out of print. Try libraries.)

A daunting, but absolutely thorough book designed to help Americans reduce legal costs after death. Dacey explains probate, trusts, and much more. Useful when preparing your own will.

Life's work

▸ Anderson, Nancy. *Work with Passion: How to Do What You Want for a Living.* New World Library, second edition, 1995.

In this inspirational but eminently practical guide, Anderson shows you how to discover and step into your ideal job. The true-life stories of ordinary people stumbling and then succeeding at work they love, are interspersed with dozens of written exercises to get you thinking — and moving.

Anderson's objective is to help you live a life that works — a life that "comes together, with a harmonious balance among all its facets: your work, your family, your loves, your finances, and your mental and spiritual growth."

Physical and emotional health

▸ Beattie, Melody. *Finding Your Way Home: A Soul Survival Kit.* HarperCollins, 1998

Following a death, you are at far greater risk than before for health and emotional problems. Beattie's book brings you "tools for discovering your emotional and spiritual power." *Finding Your Way Home* is a powerful and challenging book about buying back our souls and learning to live a live guided by spirit.

▸ Carter, Rosalynn. *Helping Yourself Help Others.* Times Books, 1996.

Drawing upon her professional and family experience, the former first lady offers advice to help caregivers deal with feelings of guilt, resentment, sadness, and burnout. Guidance is given on when to work with a health-care team, when to use support groups, and how to know when an institution is the right choice.

▸ Jampolsky, Gerald G., M.D. *Good-bye to Guilt: Releasing Fear Through Forgiveness.* Bantam Doubleday Dell, 1988.

No matter how loving the relationship, we are often left with guilt after a death ("If only I'd done more for her," or "If only I'd made him go to the doctor"). These negative emotions wreak havoc on our personal relationships, self-esteem, and peace of mind. In 14 lessons, with many real-life stories, Jampolsky shows us how to let go of fear and guilt and find inner peace — perhaps for the first time.

▸ Levine, Stephen. *Who Dies? An Investigation of Conscious Living and Conscious Dying.* Doubleday, 1989.

Levine discusses healing, pain, death at home, working with the dying, suicide, funerals, and grief. Written from a Zen Buddhist's perspective, this extraordinary book offers an opportunity for those of any faith — or no faith — to gain spiritual awakening and peace.

▸ Pearsall, Paul. *The Heart's Code: Tapping the Wisdom and Power of Our Heart Energy.* Broadway Books, 1998.

The Heart's Code is a fascinating synthesis of ancient truths, modern medicine, scientific research, and personal experience that proves that the human heart, not the brain, holds the secrets that link body, mind, and spirit. Pearsall shows that by listening to the subtle energy and wisdom each of us has within our hearts, we can learn valuable life lessons.

▸ Siegel, Bernie S., M.D. *Love, Medicine & Miracles: Lessons Learned About Self-Healing from a Surgeon's Experience with Exceptional Patients.* HarperCollins, 1990.

With many case histories, the irrepressible Dr. Siegel details his astonishing work with cancer patients. The therapy is based on "carefrontation," a loving, safe therapeutic confrontation that leads to personal change and healing. In Siegel's view, death is not a failure, since achieving a peaceful death can be a powerful form of healing.

▸ Turock, Art. *Getting Physical: How to Stick with Your Exercise Program.* Doubleday, 1989.

When coping with grief, physical exercise can lift you out of depression and give the energy to carry on. *Getting Physical* offers a progression of motivational strategies to help you design and stick to a fitness program that works for you. This is a friendly, step-by-step book written not for jocks, but for real people. Turock knows how to ignite your motivation — especially if you think you're too tired, too embarrassed, too bored, or too busy to exercise.

▸ Viscott, David, M.D., *I Love You, Let's Work It Out.* Pocket Books, 1990.

Death in the family — especially the death of a child — can produce tremendous strains on a couple. Too often, we take out our pain and anger on those who are closest to us. Dr. Viscott combines compassion and a straightforward, shoot-from-the-hip style with practical advice on now to renew your love and trust.

Burial Boxes

For those who do not wish to purchase a ready-made casket from a funeral director, Carpenter Casket Plans provides plans for homemade caskets.

▸ Send a check for $19.50 to Richard Johnstone, P.O. Box 1063, Pioneer, CA 95666. The website is *www.volcano.net/~johnstone/caskhome.html*

As well, Ernest Morgan's book, *Dealing Creatively with Death* (noted above), includes diagrams for building simple homemade burial boxes of various sizes.

Legal Expense Plans

One in five Canadians has had family disputes over inheritances and one in four expects to experience conflicts with family members over a will. Yet half of all Canadians, including many parents with children at home, have not prepared a will. Worse, seven out of ten Americans have no will. But without a will, an individual's assets are distributed according to state or provinical legislation which can mean long delays and unnecessary costs, even on a small estate. And children may be taken into public custody until guardians are identified.

Many people feel that they don't have a large enough estate to justify the cost of getting a will done. But many messy legal battles are fought over small estates, and the financial and emotional cost to survivors can be great.

I have recently discovered a legal expense plan, which provides members with a free will and many other legal protection services for a small monthly fee. First, some background . . .

Prepaid legal plans are to attorney fees what prepaid medical plans are to doctor and hospital bills. The plans are designed to help middle-income earners have affordable access to quality legal assistance. Consumers in Europe have long been familiar with this kind of legal protection. In Germany, for instance, 80% of families are covered by some form of legal insurance. In North America, although almost everyone has health coverage, very few people have a legal protection plan. Yet in 1995 alone, there were three lawsuits filed every second in the U.S. In fact, you are three times more likely to end up in court this year than in a hospital bed. Canadians are much less likely to sue, but still the courts are jammed.

Among the providers of legal protection plans, the pre-eminent firm is a publicly held, debt-free company called Pre-Paid Legal Services, Inc., headquartered in Ada, Oklahoma. The company was formed by Harland C. Stonecipher in 1972 shortly after he had a costly brush with lawyers stemming from a head-on automobile accident. Although he wasn't at fault, his legal bills accumulated rapidly. He had auto insurance, medical insurance and life insurance. The only type of protection he didn't have was for legal services.

This experience was the driving force behind Stonecipher's decision to start Pre-Paid Legal Services. He began the company with a vision to make legal protection affordable. Over the last 27 years, Pre-Paid Legal has developed the most extensive nationwide network of top-rated attorneys and law firms. In 1999 they are expanding their services to Canadians.

The typical plan, covering the entire family, costs just $25 a month and includes an umbrella of legal services, such as:

▸ Preparation of a comprehensive will (typically costing $500 and up without a plan) with free annual updates

▸ Unlimited phone calls to receive legal advice from a top-rated lawyer

▸ Review of legal documents (a young Washington woman, for instance, recently saved $7,000 over the life of her new car lease)

▸ Phone calls made and letters written on your behalf (like the elderly couple in Texas, who recovered 100% of an unfair bill for car repairs)

▸ Representation in traffic court for moving traffic violations, including your teenage drivers

▸ Representation in the case of a tragic auto accident

▸ Pre-trial and in-court legal defense

▸ Legal assistance from a certified tax attorney during a tax audit

▸ A 25% discount on all legal problems not already covered

Pre-Paid Legal takes a portion of that $25 a month membership and pays it to the top law firms in each state or province. In Oklahoma, for instance, the provider law firm receives more than $1.5 million a year. That, of course, makes each of Pre-Paid's members the firm's number one client, and as you can imagine, they receive impeccable service. When you consider that lawyers typically charge $100 to $300 an hour, just an hour or two of a lawyer's time would pay for an entire year's membership.

My husband Bob and I are so impressed with this company and its services that we have become independent Associates, helping to introduce the coverage to people all over Canada and the U.S. To find out more, you can take a look at our website at *www.equaljusticeforall.com/martin*.

Support Groups

Community service organizations, the "Y", and churches all across North America are recognizing the need to help the bereaved. Programs range from a few weekly sessions on grief, held in the church basement, to years of support and involvement in a widows' group. If you can't find what you want, call your community referral service for information about local classes and programs.

▸ **Cemetery Consumer Service Council.** P.O. Box 2028, Reston, VA 20195-0028. Phone: (703) 391-8407. Fax: (703) 391-8416.

An independent, nonprofit association created in 1979 to assist consumers in matters involving private cemeteries and memorial parks. The council helps to informally resolve consumer complaints and inquiries about cemetery services or policies. Services are available to consumers free of charge.

▸ **Centering Corporation.** 1531 N. Saddle Creek Rd, Omaha, Nebraska 68104-5064. Phone: (402) 553-1200. Fax: (402) 553-0507.

A nonprofit organization that provides a newsletter, other printed information, videos and workshops for children and parents bereaved through miscarriage, newborn death, death of older children or grandparents.

▸ **Choice in Dying.** 1035 30th Street NW, Washington, DC 20007. Phone: (202) 338-9790 or 1-800-989-9455. Fax: (202) 338-0242.

A nonprofit educational organization. Write or call for free information on the Living Will and other literature on death and dying, including patient rights and "right to die" legislation.

▸ **Compassionate Friends.** P.O. Box 3696, Oak Brook, Illinois 60522-3696. Phone: (630) 990-0010. Fax: (630) 990-0246.

An organization for the parents of children who have died. Also has information to help bereaved siblings. Call for the chapter in your area.

▸ **Internet.**

In addition to the virtual memorial pages described in chapter 14, a number of other resources can be found on the Internet. In the newsgroup called alt.support.grief, people write of their bereavement and are comforted by other subscribers. There are also pages maintained by organizations such as the Right to Die Society and even a handful of funeral homes online. Find out what's current by using a search engine to look for "death" (although this may send you to pages about heavy metal rock groups) or "death and dying" or "funeral."

▸ **Make Today Count, Inc.** (800) 432-2273 (Mid-America Cancer Center)

An international organization with over 200 chapters, for mutual support of terminally ill persons (especially cancer patients), family members, and health care professionals who need to cope with emotional problems associated with terminal illness. Offers printed material and seminars on death and dying. Call for the location of the nearest chapter.

▸ **National Association for Widowed People.** P.O. Box 3564, Springfield, Illinois 62708.

A social organization and community service for men and women of all ages who have lost a spouse. Services include a newsletter, travel club, and job service. There are 3,000 local chapters.

▸ **National Hospice Organization.** 1901 N. Moore St, Suite 901, Arlington, Virginia 22209. (703) 243-5900 or 1-800-658-8898.

Hospices provide specialized health care programs for those with terminal illness, emphasizing pain and symptom management for the patient, and emotional support of the family. NHO is the national U.S. coordinating body. Write for printed material and the Directory of Hospices in the United States.

▸ **National Self-Help Clearinghouse.** Room 620, Graduate School and University Center, City University of New York, 25 West 43rd Street, New York, NY 10036. Phone: (212) 642-2944.

A central source of information on a variety of support groups.

▸ **Parents of Murdered Children.** 100 E. 8th St., Rm. B-41, Cincinnati, Ohio 45202. Phone: (513) 721-5683.

Founded in 1978 for parents and other survivors of murder victims. Call for information, a newsletter, and the contacts for local support groups.

▸ **St. Francis Center.** 4880A MacArthur Blvd., N.W., Washington, DC 20007 Phone: (202) 333-4880. Fax: (202) 333-4540.

A nondenominational, nonprofit organization founded in 1975, to serve as a source of guidance, information and support for people living with illness, loss, and bereavement. Publishes a quarterly newsletter, "Centering" and "Living with AIDS: Perspectives for Caregivers."

▸ **Widowed Persons Service.** American Association of Retired Persons, 601 "E" Street, NW, Washington, DC 20049. Phone: (202) 434-2260. Fax: (202) 434-6474.

Provides a directory of services available for widowed people.

Definitions

Administrator A person appointed by the court to take over the role of the executor when no executor was appointed in a valid will or when there is no executor willing or able to carry out his or her duties.

Bequeathal To donate your body for use by a medical or dental school to help train future doctors and dentists, or to be used in medical research.

Burial Placing the body or cremated remains in the ground or releasing it at sea.

Committal service A service held at the graveside before the body is buried, or at the crematorium before cremation. When it is held at the graveside, this ceremony is often called the interment service.

Columbarium An arrangement of niches. The columbarium may be a wall of a room, or an entire building. It may be part of an outdoor setting — a garden wall, for instance. The columbarium itself is constructed of long-lasting materials such as bronze, marble, granite, brick, stone, or concrete.

Cremains A term used in the cremation industry to mean the cremated remains.

Cremation A method of disposition whereby the body is placed in a special furnace or chamber and subjected to temperatures of up to 2,000 degrees F. for several hours. The intense heat and evaporation reduce the body to between three and nine pounds of "ash" and bone fragments.

Crypt A tomb for above-ground burial of the body.

Disposition The final handling of the deceased's remains. The two choices for disposition are burial and cremation, with many variations on each.

Embalming Injecting the body with fluids that will temporarily preserve it from decay, until after the viewing or funeral service.

Entombment	Above-ground burial; placing the body in a crypt in a mausoleum.
Estate	All real property (land and buildings) and personal possessions of the deceased as well as any liabilities.
Executor	The personal representative of the deceased as appointed in a legal will. The executor has the authority to take temporary legal ownership and possession of all the deceased's assets, to buy and sell property and possessions, and to divide up the estate among the beneficiaries.
Funeral service	A service in which the body is present. The casket may be open or closed. Following the funeral service, the body is buried or cremated.
Grave Liner	A wood or concrete box (or concrete sections that are fitted together to form an enclosure) to hold the casket.
Interment	Burial of the body in the ground.
Living Will	A signed, dated, and witnessed document that allows you to state in advance your wishes about the use of life-sustaining procedures when you are dying.
Mausoleum	A large structure, often on the grounds of a cemetery, containing one or more crypts.
Memorial park	A cemetery in which the markers are set flush with the ground to make it easier to mow the lawns.
Memorial service	A service in which the body is not present. The body may be buried or cremated, and disposition may take place before or after the service.
Memorial Society	A nonprofit, nonsectarian organization of laypeople whose purpose is "to assure dignity, simplicity, and economy in funeral arrangements, through advance planning."
Memorialization	A term used by people in the cremation industry to encourage people not to see cremation as an end in itself, but only a prelude to choosing a niche, crypt, or burial of the cremated remains.
Niche	A recessed compartment in a columbarium. The niche may be open-front, protected by glass, or a closed ornamental front, faced with bronze, marble, or granite. The urn containing the cremated remains (or some other memento of the person) is placed inside the niche and the front is sealed.
Obituary	Notice of death in a newspaper.

Pall

A cloth that covers the casket.

Probate

The legal process of proving before the courts that a particular Will is the genuine Last Will and Testament of the deceased. Granting of probate does not mean that the Will has been declared valid.

Right of Survivorship

An agreement made with a financial institution when a joint account is opened that lets the survivor continue to draw money from the joint account after the death of the partner.

Urn

A small vase-like container that holds the cremated remains. Urns come in many sizes, shapes, and materials.

Vault

A two-part casket enclosure, made of reinforced concrete with a non-porous lining (such as asphalt) or galvanized metal (such as stainless steel or copper). Sometimes called a lawn crypt.

Viewing

When the casket is open so that mourners may take a last look at the deceased.

Visitation

When the body is laid out in a casket (which may be open or closed) before the service so that mourners may come to "visit" with the deceased and the family.

Wake

A reception held by family or friends the night of the death or after the funeral or memorial service.

Will

A written document, legally executed, by which a person determines the disposal of his or her estate after death.

Permissions

Acknowledgment is made for kind permission to print the following excerpts:

Excerpts from ANN LANDERS columns which appeared in *The Chicago Tribune.* Permission granted by Ann Landers and Creators Syndicate.

Excerpts from DEALING CREATIVELY WITH DEATH by Ernest Morgan. Copyright © 1988 and 1994. Used by permission of Celo Press and Zinn Communications.

Excerpt from ESTABLISHING A PRIVATE FOUNDATION by Wolfe Goodman and Howard Carr. Reproduced with permission from The Canadian Centre for Philanthropy, © 1987.

Excerpts from WHO DIES? by Stephen Levine. Copyright © 1982 by Stephen Levine. Used by permission of Doubleday, a division of Bantam, Doubleday, Dell Publishing Group, Inc.

About the Author

Award-winning writer Sheila Martin lives with her husband, Bob, and cats Boomer and Bambi, in a home on the ocean in White Rock, British Columbia. Sheila and her sister, Toni Alain, coauthored a cookbook called *Food from the Heart*. She holds an honors degree in sociology from Simon Fraser University.

This book grew out of Sheila's own experiences looking after the details following four deaths in her own family. She hopes that owning a copy of *Saying Goodbye* will be like having a knowledgeable, highly organized friend by your side, helping you through the crisis.

Sheila invites you to visit her website at *www.equaljusticeforall.com/martin*

Index

C

D

Y

The Tool Kit

If you are a list-maker, the Tool Kit will give you a ready-made set of forms on which to list important information. You are welcome to make photocopies of any of these forms for your own use. The forms include

1   Accommodation Plans

2   Collecting Cash and Benefits

3   Day of the Service

4   Death Certificate Information

5   Gifts Received

6   Information for Callers

7   People to Call Right Away

8   People to Notify Later

9   Phone Calls Log

10 Questions for the Funeral Director

11 Service Arrangements

12 To Do List

13 Travel Plans

14 Visitors Log

▸ Accommodation Plans

Use this sheet to keep track of arrivals, departures, and accommodation arrangements for out-of-town visitors.

Names	ARR ·date	DEP date	Staying at	Arranged by	Notes

©1999, Sheila Martin

▸ Collecting Cash and Benefits

Use this sheet to keep track of your efforts to collect monies owing to the estate. Use a separate sheet for each amount due.

SOURCE OF CASH OR BENEFIT	Amount: $
Account # / Policy #	
Contact Name	**Phone #**
Notes	

ACTION RECORD

Date	Action Taken	Follow-up Required	OK
			☐
			☐
			☐
			☐
			☐
			☐
			☐
			☐
			☐
			☐
			☐
			☐
			☐

▸ Day of the Service

Use this sheet to draw up a schedule or "to do" list for the day of the service. Include information such as who is traveling in which cars, time of departure for the service, and preparations for the reception.

Schedule / "To Do" List
☐
☐
☐
☐
☐
☐
☐
☐
☐
☐
☐
☐
☐
☐
☐
☐
☐
☐
☐
☐
☐
☐
☐
☐
☐

▸ Death Certificate Information

Use this sheet to record information that will be needed for the death certificate. (The information required in your jurisdiction may be slightly different from what is here.) Take it with you when you meet with the doctor or funeral director or whoever will be helping you complete the registration of death form.

Full name	
Residence address	
Lived in this location since	
Birthplace	**Birthdate**
Citizenship	**Marital status**
Name of Spouse	**Place and date of marriage**
Name and birthplace of father	
Birth name and birthplace of mother	
Usual occupation	**Kind of business or industry**
Social Security / Social Insurance Number	
If a veteran, rank and branch of service	**Serial no.**
Date and place entered service	
Date discharged	

©1999, Sheila Martin

▶ Gifts Received

Use this sheet to record memorial donations and flowers, even gifts of food that you receive.

Date received	Description	From	Acknowledged
			☐
			☐
			☐
			☐
			☐
			☐
			☐
			☐
			☐
			☐
			☐
			☐
			☐
			☐
			☐
			☐
			☐
			☐
			☐
			☐
			☐
			☐
			☐
			☐
			☐

▶ Information for Callers

Keep this sheet near the phone so you will be able to give complete and accurate information to all callers.

Information about the death (place, time, cause, age)

Information about the visitation (date, time, place, viewing, ceremony)

Information about the service (date, time, place, viewing or not, type of service)

Information about the burial or cremation (date, time, place, type of ceremony)

Information about the wake or reception (date, time, place, parking)

Special requests (for example, memorial instead of flowers)

©1999, Sheila Martin

▶ People to Call Right Away

Use this sheet to list people to be called right away: immediate family, close friends, and all who are to be invited to the service.

Name	Phone Number	Contacted
		❑
		❑
		❑
		❑
		❑
		❑
		❑
		❑
		❑
		❑
		❑
		❑
		❑
		❑
		❑
		❑
		❑
		❑
		❑
		❑
		❑
		❑
		❑
		❑
		❑

▸ People to Notify Later

Use this sheet to record the names of people you will contact (by phone, or letter) sometime after the service.

Name	Phone Number	Address	Notified
			☐
			☐
			☐
			☐
			☐
			☐
			☐
			☐
			☐
			☐
			☐
			☐
			☐
			☐
			☐
			☐
			☐
			☐
			☐
			☐
			☐
			☐
			☐
			☐

©1999, Sheila Martin

Saying Goodbye with Love

▶ Phone Calls Log

Use this sheet to keep track of who you have called, who has called you, and a brief note about the conversation.

Date	To / From	Notes

▶ Questions for the Funeral Director

Use this sheet to make a list of questions or requests you want to discuss with the funeral director.

Question or Request	Funeral Director's Response

▶ Service Arrangements

Use this sheet to record information about the funeral or memorial service.

❑ **Funeral service**	❑ **Memorial Service**	❑ **Other**

Date	**Time**
Place	
Contact Person	**Phone #**
Presiding at Service	**Phone #**
Pallbearers	
Eulogist	**Musicians**

Program

Special Arrangements

Viewing and Visitation Arrangements

Flowers

Reception Arrangements

▶ To Do List

See chapter 3 for items that could be included on this list.

Description	Assigned to (name)	Complete by (date/time)	Done
			❏
			❏
			❏
			❏
			❏
			❏
			❏
			❏
			❏
			❏
			❏
			❏
			❏
			❏
			❏
			❏
			❏
			❏
			❏
			❏
			❏
			❏
			❏
			❏
			❏
			❏
			❏

▶ Travel Plans

If you have out-of-town visitors, use this sheet to record travel plans.

Traveler	Arrival Date / Time	Arriving At	To Be Met By	Departure Date / Time	To Be Taken to Airport By

‣ Visitors Log

Use this sheet to keep track of visitors, perhaps noting offers of help, or special things you want to remember.

Date	Visitor	Notes